Mastering Problem Solving, Enhances Mental Health, Personal Growth, and Resilience.

By Belladonna Sterling

"Mastering Problem-Solving for Enhanced Mental Health, Personal Growth, and Resilience."

This book is a work of nonfiction. The views and opinions expressed in this book are those of the author and do not necessarily reflect the official policy or position of any organization or entity mentioned within.

Table of Content

Introduction: 8
The Crucial Role of Mastering Problem-Solving for Enhanced Mental
Health and Personal Growth   11
The Transformative Power of Problem-Solving Skills   16
Problem-solving skills   28
Developing problem-solving skills   37
Chapter 1: The Foundation of Resilience: Understanding
Problem-Solving   43
    Section 1: The Essence of Resilience   43
    Section 2: The Role of Problem-Solving   50
    Section 3: Problem-Solving for Resilience   56
Chapter 2: Navigating Life's Labyrinth: The Problem-Solving Mindset
68
    "The Enchanted Labyrinth of Wisdom"   68
    Section 1: Cultivating the Problem-Solving Mindset   71
    Section 2: The Creative Problem-Solving Process   76
    Section 3: The Creative Spark: Generating Solutions   108
    Section 4: Implementing Solutions with Precision   125
Chapter 3: Resilience, Stress, and Problem-Solving   134
    Section 1: The Stress-Resilience Connection   134
    Section 2: Problem-Solving as a Stress Reduction Tool   140
    Section 3: Building Resilience through Problem-Solving 146
Chapter 4: Empowerment through Problem-Solving: Taking Control of
Your Journey   157
    Section 1: The Path to Empowerment   157
    Section 2: Developing Empowering Problem-Solving Skills 162
    Section 3: The Journey to Self-Belief   168
    Section 4: Applying Empowerment to Life's Challenges   174
Chapter 5: Mastering the Art of Problem Solving   181
    Section 1: Identifying and Defining the Problem   182
    Section 2: Generating Creative Solutions   186
    Section 3: Evaluating and Choosing the Best Solution   188
    Section 4: Implementation and Continuous Improvement   190
    Section 5: Evaluating the Outcome and Continuous Learning 193

Section 6: Seeking Guidance and Building Expertise 196

Section 7: Embracing Problem-Solving as a Way of Life 198

Section 8: Inspiring Others and Leaving a Legacy 201

Section 9: The Lifelong Journey of Problem Solving 204

Chapter Conclusion: A Lifelong Pursuit of Mastery 205

Chapter 6: Building Self-Confidence and Overcoming Fear through Problem Solving 206

Section 1: The Connection Between Problem-Solving and Self-Confidence 206

Section 2: Overcoming Fear with Problem-Solving 207

Section 3: Practical Problem-Solving for Confidence and Fearlessness 212

Section 4: The Journey Ahead 218

Section 1: The Connection Between Problem-Solving and Self-Confidence 218

Section 2: Overcoming Fear with Problem-Solving 219

Section 3: Practical Problem-Solving for Confidence and Fearlessness 221

Section 4: The Journey Ahead 222

Chapter 7: Problem-Solving for Enhanced Mental Well-Being 225

Section 1: The Intersection of Problem-Solving and Mental Health 226

Section 2: Building Resilience through Problem-Solving 232

Section 3: Practical Problem-Solving for Mental Wellness 237

Section 4: Navigating Life's Challenges 241

Chapter 8: Building Resilience and Adaptation in the Face of Change 248

Section 1: Understanding Resilience 248

Section 2: Building Resilience 249

Section 3: Adaptation and Coping Skills 252

Section 4: Thriving in a Changing World 254

Section 5: Embracing Creativity 256

Section 6: Conclusion and Transition to Chapter 9 258

Chapter 9: Evaluating Self-Efforts, Learning from Results, and Cultivating Mental Health and Self-Sufficiency 261

Section 1: Assessing Self-Efforts and Results 261

Section 2: Learning from the Process   263

Section 3: Mental Health Improvement and Self-Sufficiency   264

Section 4: Applying Your Learnings   266

Section 5: Personal Growth and Transformation   268

Chapter 10: Empowering Change Agents   **272**

Section 1: The Power of Collective Problem Solving   272

Section 2: Case Studies and Examples   273

Section 3: Ethical Responsibilities   274

Section 4: Contributions to Mental Health and Personal Growth   276

Section 5: Becoming Change Agents   277

Section 6: Navigating Challenges   279

Section 7: Measuring Impact and Celebrating Success   280

Section 8: Conclusion and Call to Action   282

Chapter 11: The Journey Ahead - Sustaining Growth and Impact   **284**

Section 1: Sustaining Personal Growth   284

Section 2: Expanding Your Impact   293

Section 3: Nurturing Resilience   295

Section 4: Conclusion and Looking Forward   303

Chapter 12: Leaving a Lasting Legacy   **307**

Section 1: The Ripple Effect of Your Actions   307

Section 2: Strategies for Mentoring and Empowering Future Change
Agents   308

Section 3: Reflecting on Your Journey   310

Section 4: Conclusion and Your Ongoing Legacy   311

Chapter 13: Conclusion and Your Ongoing Journey   **312**

Section 1: Reflecting on Your Journey   312

Section 2: Your Ongoing Journey   314

Section 3: Paying It Forward   315

Section 4: Final Thoughts and Farewell   317

Chapter 14: Developing Critical Thinking Skills   **319**

Section 1: Understanding Critical Thinking   319

Section 2: Developing Critical Thinking Skills   343

Section 3: Problem-Solving and Decision-Making   357

Section 4: Conclusion and Ongoing Practice   371

Author's Final Words   377

Today, make the choice to *thrive* and *grow*.
THE UNIVERSE

Introduction:

In the grand tapestry of life, there exists a universal truth: challenges and obstacles are woven into the very fabric of our existence. From the complexities of our personal relationships to the ever-evolving landscape of our professional pursuits, the ability to navigate these challenges with grace and resilience is the hallmark of a life well-lived. Welcome to "Mastering Problem-Solving for Enhanced Mental Health, Personal Growth, and Resilience," a book that encapsulates the wisdom and insights I've gained as a dedicated practitioner in the realm of mental health and problem-solving.

As the author of this book, I've had the privilege of accompanying countless individuals on their unique journeys towards personal growth and mental well-being. Throughout my years in practice, I've come to understand that the art of effective problem-solving is intrinsically intertwined with the cultivation of robust mental health and the fostering of personal growth. Just as we nurture our physical health, our minds require attention, care, and skillful guidance to flourish in the face of life's challenges.

Within the pages of this book, I invite you to embark on a transformative journey through the realms of problem-solving and mental well-being. Together, we will delve into the intricate connections between our cognitive processes, the obstacles we encounter, and the profound influence these factors exert on our emotional and psychological landscapes.

In the chapters that follow, we will explore a comprehensive framework for mastering the art of problem-solving, informed by the latest insights from psychology and neuroscience, as well as the practical knowledge honed through my clinical practice. This framework will not only equip you with the tools to conquer challenges in any domain of life but also empower you to harness problem-solving as a potent catalyst for personal growth and mental resilience.

Additionally, our voyage will encompass mindfulness techniques, stress management strategies, and self-care practices, all of which are indispensable for nurturing and safeguarding your mental well-being. By intertwining these practices with the art of problem-solving, you will forge a powerful alliance between your mental health, personal growth, and resilience.

As we journey through these pages together, my aspiration is for you to emerge not only as a proficient problem solver but also as a steward of your own mental landscape. By the culmination of this book, I aim for you to possess a profound understanding of problem-solving as a pathway to enhanced mental health and personal growth, equipped with an arsenal of strategies and insights to navigate life's labyrinth with unwavering confidence, unwavering resilience, and unbounded potential.

So, let us embark on this expedition of self-discovery, problem-solving mastery, and the cultivation of mental well-being. In the chapters that unfold, you will discover the keys to unlocking your innate capacity for personal growth, enhanced mental health, and unwavering resilience—the keys to a life lived to its fullest potential.

The Crucial Role of Mastering Problem-Solving for Enhanced Mental Health and Personal Growth

Imagine life as a labyrinth, full of twists, turns, and unexpected challenges. Navigating this intricate maze, one often encounters barriers that threaten to halt progress and shroud the path ahead in uncertainty. It is within this intricate web of experiences that we discover the true significance of problem-solving skills—a dynamic set of tools that hold the power to illuminate the way forward.

In the journey of "Mastering Problem-Solving for Enhanced Mental Health and Personal Growth," we find ourselves at a crossroads, poised to delve into the profound interplay between resilience, personal growth, and the art of problem solving. Each of these facets of our existence is inextricably linked, like threads in the fabric of our lives.

Resilience Building: Picture resilience as the profound ability to withstand life's tempests without losing one's inner light. When trials and tribulations strike, we find ourselves at a fork in the road. Some may yield to adversity, while others rise to the occasion, propelled by the force of resilience. It is through problem-solving that this resilience is forged—like steel tempered in the crucible of life's challenges. Every problem tackled becomes a stepping stone, each setback a lesson, and the process of solving becomes a crucible for resilience.

Stress Reduction: Along this labyrinthine journey, we often encounter stress, that relentless companion of adversity. It lurks in the shadows, ready to seize our tranquility. However, with problem-solving skills as our lantern, we can pierce the darkness. Problems, once enigmatic and overwhelming, become puzzles to be solved. We dissect them, break them down into manageable fragments, and in doing so, we diminish their power to induce stress. With structured problem-solving, the formidable transforms into the familiar.

Empowerment: At the heart of this journey is empowerment—a transformative force that bestows upon us a sense of control over our destinies. When we approach life's challenges with the mindset of a problem solver, we cease to be passive spectators and become active participants in our own narratives. The act of resolving problems becomes a declaration of self-belief—an affirmation that we possess the capacity to shape our circumstances. It is through the lens of problem-solving that we discover our inner strength, foster self-confidence, and become the architects of our own destinies.

Adaptability: The journey is fluid, ever-changing, and filled with unpredictability. In such an environment, adaptability is a cherished skill. Effective problem solvers have an innate capacity to pivot and adjust their strategies as the terrain shifts beneath their feet. This adaptability is not merely a survival tool; it is the cornerstone of personal growth. By embracing change and learning from new experiences, we refine our resilience and continuously evolve.

Goal Achievement: Goals—be they personal, professional, or in the realm of mental well-being—are the beacons guiding us through the labyrinth. They represent our aspirations and ambitions. Yet, the path to goal achievement is often riddled with obstacles. Here, problem-solving skills shine as beacons of their own. They enable us to surmount barriers, overcome challenges, and bridge the chasm between where we are and where we wish to be.

Emotional Regulation: Emotions, like tempestuous winds, can threaten to unmoor us from our course. But problem-solving provides the anchor—a rational approach that steadies the ship. When faced with adversity, problem solvers confront it with a cool, analytical eye. This mindset mitigates the turbulence of negative emotions, preserving the equilibrium of mental well-being.

Conflict Resolution: Life is a tapestry of relationships, and where there are relationships, there are conflicts. In the pursuit of mental well-being and personal growth, harmonious interactions are vital. Problem solvers possess a unique skill set that transcends personal interests, allowing them to navigate conflicts with finesse. They find common ground, build bridges, and cultivate relationships that are a source of strength.

Continuous Learning: The journey is a journey of continuous learning—a voyage that stretches our horizons and enriches our understanding. With each problem we encounter, we gain insights, acquire new skills, and expand our knowledge. This process of continuous learning is the lifeblood of personal growth, fostering a growth mindset and nurturing a sense of curiosity.

As we set forth on this transformative journey through the pages of"Mastering Problem-Solving for Enhanced Mental Health and Personal Growth" we do so with an understanding that problem-solving skills are not mere tools for overcoming obstacles. They are the very fabric of our empowerment, resilience, and growth. By honing these skills, we illuminate the path forward, reduce the shadows of uncertainty, and reveal the potential that resides within.

Are you ready to embrace this journey—a journey where resilience, personal growth, and problem-solving intertwine to empower you to thrive in the labyrinth of life? The adventure unfolds, and your inner resilience awaits its awakening.

Welcome to the transformative world of "Mastering Problem-Solving for Enhanced Mental Health and Personal Growth"

"Life is 10% what happens to us and 90% how we react to it." —Charles R. Swindoll

The Transformative Power of Problem-Solving Skills

Now that we've illuminated the profound connection between problem-solving skills, resilience, personal growth, and mental well-being, let's dive deeper into the transformative power that these skills hold within the context of our lives. Each facet of this transformation is a milestone on our journey towards unleashing our inner resilience and unlocking our potential for personal growth and mental well-being.

Resilience Amplification:

• Resilience Amplification: In the intricate dance of life, adversity and challenges are inevitable partners. However, the true measure of our resilience lies not in the absence of difficulties but in our response to them. Much like a blacksmith tempers steel in a fiery forge, our resilience is forged in the crucible of life's trials.

• Our ability to navigate and conquer these obstacles is intrinsically tied to our problem-solving skills. These skills are not mere tools in our toolkit; they are the sparks that ignite our inner strength. With each challenge we confront head-on, we not only overcome it but also emerge from the ordeal with newfound vigor and fortitude.

• Think of resilience as a muscle, one that grows and strengthens with each exercise. The more we apply our problem-solving prowess to life's intricate puzzles, the more robust our resilience becomes. It becomes a wellspring of inner strength, a source of unwavering determination that propels us forward, even in the face of the unknown.

• As we amplify our resilience, we transcend the role of mere survivors. We become thrivers, individuals who not only weather life's storms but harness their power for personal growth and transformation. Resilience is not just about bouncing back; it's about bouncing forward, stronger, and more prepared for the challenges that lie ahead.

• In this journey of resilience amplification, we'll explore the art of problem-solving as a catalyst for personal growth and mental well-being. Together, we'll unlock the secrets to not only overcoming life's adversities but also using them as stepping stones towards a future filled with unwavering determination, boundless strength, and the unshakable belief that we can thrive in the face of any challenge.

Stress as a Catalyst for Growth:

• Stress as a Catalyst for Growth: Stress, often seen as an unwelcome adversary on our life's journey, possesses a hidden potential waiting to be unlocked through the power of problem-solving. Instead of succumbing to stress, we have the capacity to harness its energy and redirect its formidable force.

• With each problem we confront and successfully solve, we not only diminish the weight of stress but transform it into a potent source of motivation. It's a profound shift in perspective—a metamorphosis of stress from a burden that weighs us down into a dynamic force that propels us towards personal development.

• In this transformation, we discover that stress is not merely an obstacle but a crucible for growth. Like a crucible that refines metals, stress can refine our character, strengthen our resilience, and sharpen our problem-solving skills. It becomes the crucible of transformation where we forge our inner resolve, emerging from the fires of adversity stronger, wiser, and more determined.

• As we navigate life's challenges with a problem-solving mindset, stress evolves from an impediment to a catalyst. It fuels our journey, acting as a driving force that compels us to push beyond our limits, explore new horizons, and achieve personal growth milestones we once deemed unattainable.

• So, let us embark on this transformative journey together, where we learn to not only cope with stress but to embrace it as a catalyst for our own evolution. Through problem-solving, we will unveil the latent potential within stress, unlocking a wellspring of motivation that propels us towards a future filled with personal growth, resilience, and the unwavering belief that we can thrive, no matter the circumstances.

The Empowered Mindset:

• The Empowered Mindset: Empowerment is not a transient sensation; it is a mindset that takes root and thrives through the active cultivation of problem-solving skills. As we navigate the intricate tapestry of life's challenges, we cultivate a deep-seated belief in our ability to enact change. This newfound belief is a profound transformation that reshapes our entire outlook on life.

• With each problem we confront and solve, we reinforce our conviction that we possess the agency to shape our destiny. This belief becomes the cornerstone of our empowered mindset, and it has far-reaching effects on our well-being. It breeds self-confidence, bolsters our determination, and becomes the driving force behind our pursuit of personal growth and mental well-being.

• The empowered mindset is not merely a state of mind; it is an active force that propels us forward. It compels us to take initiative, set ambitious goals, and confront life's challenges with unwavering resolve. It allows us to view setbacks not as failures but as opportunities for growth and learning.

• As we embark on this journey of empowerment through problem-solving, we will uncover the incredible capacity within us to effect positive change in our lives and the lives of others. The empowered mindset, once cultivated, becomes a wellspring of strength, resilience, and boundless potential. Together, we will harness the power of problem-solving to nurture this mindset and propel ourselves towards a future brimming with personal growth and mental well-being.

Adapting to Life's Flux:

Adapting to Life's Flux: Life is an intricate tapestry woven with the threads of change, and at its core lies the profound concept of adaptability. Effective problem solvers not only comprehend but embrace the idea that change is not an insurmountable obstacle; it is an extraordinary opportunity.

With each twist and turn on the journey of life, they greet change with open arms, recognizing that it carries the promise of new experiences, fresh perspectives, and the cultivation of unyielding resilience. In this ever-evolving world, adaptability, coupled with the power of problem-solving, serves as our guiding compass, navigating us through uncharted waters.

Just as a skilled sailor adjusts their sails to harness the wind's power, adept problem solvers adjust their strategies to harness the winds of change. They thrive in an environment where others falter because they possess the ability to pivot gracefully, leveraging their problem-solving skills to surmount unforeseen challenges.

In the face of adversity, they do not merely survive; they thrive. They are the architects of their destinies, architects who construct resilience as they encounter life's ebb and flow. Adaptability through problem-solving is not just a skill; it's a way of life, a philosophy that propels us to not only weather life's storms but to emerge from them stronger, wiser, and more empowered.

Together, we embark on a transformative journey where adaptability and problem-solving are our steadfast companions. As we navigate the ever-shifting seas of existence, may we draw inspiration from the art of adaptability, using it to craft a future rich in personal growth, mental well-being, and the unshakable belief that we can not only endure change but flourish within it.

Turning Goals into Reality:

• Goals, regardless of their scale, serve as essential signposts along the path of personal growth. Yet, these aspirations are often elusive dreams until the power of problem-solving comes into play. With these problem-solving skills at our disposal, we possess the alchemical ability to transmute these goals from distant fantasies into concrete, achievable realities.

• Approaching our aspirations with a systematic problem-solving mindset, we do more than merely wish for their realization; we actively diminish the barriers that stand in their way. Each challenge becomes an opportunity for innovation and determination, rather than a roadblock. As we tackle these obstacles systematically and with purpose, we steadily advance towards our cherished goals, marking our progress on the map of our personal growth journey.

• Consider each goal as a destination on a remarkable voyage, and problem-solving as the compass guiding our way. With each step, we bring these goals closer, until they are no longer just ethereal ideals but tangible achievements. Through this transformative process, we redefine our sense of what's possible, taking our first steps towards a more fulfilling, empowered life.

• Together, let's embark on this transformative journey where the power of problem-solving serves as the catalyst for turning aspirations into reality. As we strive to conquer challenges systematically, may we find fulfillment in every milestone achieved, and may we use the momentum of our progress to propel us towards a life filled with personal growth, purpose, and the unwavering belief that our dreams are well within reach.

A Tranquil Mind Amidst Chaos:

- Amidst the tempestuous sea of life's trials and tribulations, emotional regulation stands as our unwavering anchor, ensuring that we remain steady and resolute. Problem-solving, we discover, is not merely an intellectual endeavor; it is an emotional journey as well.

- As we confront life's myriad challenges armed with a rational, solution-oriented mindset, we find ourselves navigating the stormy waters of our emotions with remarkable grace. The turmoil within us, once an unyielding tempest, begins to yield to the steady hand of our problem-solving prowess. Emotional upheaval gives way to a tranquil mind, and we learn the art of riding the waves of our feelings with poise and wisdom.

- In this transformative process, emotional stability becomes the cornerstone of our mental well-being. It's not about suppressing our emotions but understanding them, acknowledging their presence, and responding to them with empathy and insight. We embrace the power of problem-solving as a means to not only resolve external challenges but to cultivate inner peace.

- Together, we embark on a profound journey where emotional regulation and problem-solving are the allies that guide us through life's chaos. As we navigate the turbulent sea of emotions, may we find solace in the serenity of our minds and the assurance that mental well-being is not just an aspiration but a tangible reality we can achieve.

Building Bridges to Harmony:

- Within the intricate tapestry of our lives, relationships are the vibrant threads that weave the story of our existence. Yet, conflicts, like shadows, occasionally cast their presence across these relationships. However, embedded within the fabric of problem-solving lies the power to transform conflicts into fertile soil for personal and interpersonal growth.

- Through the lens of problem-solving, we acquire the wisdom to view conflicts not as insurmountable barriers but as opportunities waiting to be unearthed. With empathy as our guide, we embark on a journey towards resolution, seeking common ground with the fervor of explorers and building bridges of understanding that connect the hearts and minds of those involved.

- As we cultivate this skill, our relationships evolve into sacred sanctuaries of mutual respect and compassion. Conflicts become the crucibles in which we forge stronger connections, deepen our understanding of one another, and lay the foundations of trust and harmony. These healthy relationships become the steadfast pillars upon which we lean in times of need, providing unwavering support and contributing to our overall mental well-being.

- Together, we embark on this transformative journey where problem-solving skills become the catalysts for building bridges to harmony within our relationships. As we navigate the occasional storms of conflict with empathy as our compass, may we discover that beneath the surface of discord lies the potential for deeper connection, growth, and relationships that serve as enduring sources of strength and well-being.

The Quest for Knowledge:

- Our life's journey is an ever-unfolding narrative of continuous learning. In the tapestry of existence, each problem we encounter is not just a challenge to overcome but a gateway to knowledge and wisdom. Through the lens of problem-solving, we don't merely seek solutions; we embark on a quest for understanding.

- Problem-solving serves as the artisan's chisel, carefully carving the sculpture of a growth mindset within us. This mindset is marked by an insatiable thirst for knowledge and a deep-rooted curiosity that knows no bounds. It is a mindset that propels us forward, encouraging us to not only conquer the challenges at hand but to actively seek out new challenges, explore uncharted territories, and, in the process, transform into lifelong learners.

- With each problem solved, we add another layer to our intellectual and emotional depth. We become the architects of our own education; our curiosity is the compass guiding our course. This quest for knowledge becomes a lifelong odyssey, a journey of self-discovery, and a testament to the transformative power of problem-solving.

- Together, we embark on this noble journey where problem-solving is our trusty companion, leading us toward a future illuminated by the ever-glowing torch of knowledge. As we navigate life's intricacies with a growth mindset, may we inspire in ourselves and others an unwavering commitment to the pursuit of wisdom, ensuring that our journey remains an endless quest for knowledge and self-improvement.

As we progress through this transformative exploration of problem-solving, remember that these skills are not abstract concepts but active agents of change in our lives. They are the compass, the lantern, and the sail that guide us, illuminate our path, and propel us forward. Problem-solving is not just a means to an end; it is the catalyst for our growth, the cornerstone of our resilience, and the linchpin of our mental well-being.

Are you ready to embrace the transformative power of problem-solving skills—a power that will shape your journey towards resilience, personal growth, and mental well-being? As we delve deeper into this transformative journey, each step will bring us closer to unleashing our inner resilience and embracing a life filled with growth and well-being.

Problem-solving skills

Problem-solving skills are fundamental to the journey of "Mastering Problem-Solving for Enhanced Mental Health and Personal Growth." These skills serve as powerful tools that enable individuals to navigate life's challenges, adapt to adversity, and cultivate the inner strength needed to thrive. Here's why problem-solving skills are so crucial in this context:

Resilience Building: At the heart of resilience lies a powerful connection to problem-solving. When individuals encounter the formidable obstacles that life can present, they stand at a crossroads. They can choose to yield to these challenges or embark on a journey of problem-solving to conquer them. It's in this pivotal choice that the seeds of resilience are sown.

The development of effective problem-solving skills becomes the mighty tool that empowers individuals to defy adversity. With each challenge confronted and solved, the resilience within them grows like a steadfast tree, weathering the harshest of storms. It is through the fires of adversity and the crucible of problem-solving that their inner strength is forged and fortified.

Resilience, therefore, is not merely the ability to endure; it is the art of bouncing back from setbacks, strengthened and renewed. It's the embodiment of the indomitable spirit that refuses to be defeated. Through the lens of problem-solving, resilience becomes the guiding star, leading the way through the darkest of times and inspiring individuals to rise above their circumstances.

Together, we embark on this profound journey where problem-solving serves as the cornerstone of resilience building. As we confront challenges head-on, may we find the resilience within ourselves to not only weather life's storms but to emerge from them with newfound strength and the unshakable belief that we can thrive, no matter the circumstances.

Stress Reduction: Life's challenges and setbacks often act as the kindling for the flames of stress. Yet, within the realm of problem-solving, individuals discover a powerful tool for dousing these flames. It's a tool that enables them to not only confront challenges head-on but also to reduce the levels of stress that can engulf them.

Problem-solving, in its structured and systematic form, serves as a calming balm for the anxious mind. It allows individuals to deconstruct complex problems into their constituent parts, transforming what seemed insurmountable into manageable components. This process of dissection and analysis brings clarity and structure to chaos, rendering challenges less daunting.

In the face of adversity, problem-solving becomes the compass that guides individuals through the labyrinth of stress. It provides a tangible path forward, helping to dispel the overwhelming feelings of helplessness and uncertainty. By breaking down problems into manageable fragments, problem-solving allows individuals to regain a sense of control over their lives.

Together, we embark on this transformative journey where problem-solving becomes the antidote to stress. As we confront life's challenges with a structured mindset, may we find solace in the knowledge that stress need not hold us captive. With problem-solving as our ally, we can reduce its grip on our lives and rediscover a sense of calm and equilibrium amidst the tumultuous sea of adversity.

Empowerment: Within the realm of problem-solving lies the profound gift of empowerment. It is the essence of taking control over one's own life, a vital facet of personal growth and mental well-being. As individuals actively engage in addressing and resolving life's challenges, they experience a transformation—an awakening of inner strength.

Problem-solving bestows upon individuals a profound sense of agency. It grants them the power to steer the course of their lives, not as passive spectators but as active participants. Through the act of confronting and conquering challenges, they foster a deep-seated belief in their own capabilities. This newfound belief is the cornerstone of empowerment, a quality that fuels self-confidence and imbues them with a profound sense of purpose.

Empowerment is not just a state of mind; it is a force of nature that propels individuals forward on their journey of personal growth. With each problem solved, they reinforce their conviction that they have the power to shape their destiny. This conviction becomes the fuel that ignites their determination to pursue mental well-being and personal development.

Together, we embark on this transformative journey where problem-solving becomes the catalyst for empowerment. As we actively address and resolve life's challenges, may we uncover the wellspring of strength within us and cultivate the unwavering belief that we possess the power to not only endure but to thrive in the face of adversity.

Adaptability: In the ever-changing tapestry of life, adaptability is the golden thread that weaves resilience into its very fabric. It's the ability to not only weather the storms of change but also to dance in the rain. At the heart of adaptability lies the core of problem-solving, and it is this synergy that equips individuals to navigate the shifting tides of existence.

Life, like a chameleon, constantly changes its colors and patterns, and effective problem solvers are its skilled artists. They possess the remarkable talent to adjust their strategies and approaches as circumstances evolve. This adaptability is the secret to not only surviving change but also thriving within it.

Through the lens of problem-solving, adaptability becomes the key to personal growth. It is the willingness to embrace the unfamiliar, to step into uncharted territories, and to learn from each new experience. This adaptability is the gateway to a life rich with learning, expansion, and the relentless pursuit of self-improvement.

Together, we embark on a transformative journey where adaptability and problem-solving stand as our guiding stars. As we adjust our sails to the winds of change, may we discover the boundless potential that resides within us, and may we embrace change as an ally rather than an adversary on our path to personal growth and resilience.

Goal Achievement: In the grand tapestry of life, goals are the shimmering stars that guide our journey. Yet, it is the art of problem-solving that acts as the compass, helping us chart a course towards these celestial aspirations. Problem-solving skills are the bridge that transforms dreams into tangible achievements.

Each goal, whether it be a personal quest for self-improvement, a professional ambition for career advancement, or a vital step towards mental well-being, is an opportunity for growth. However, the path to these goals is often strewn with obstacles and challenges. It is here that problem-solving skills come to the forefront, empowering us to overcome these hurdles and forge ahead.

Problem-solving equips us with the tools needed to navigate the labyrinthine journey towards goal achievement. It is the flashlight that illuminates the darkest corners, revealing hidden solutions and pathways. With each obstacle surmounted, we inch closer to our cherished goals, marking our progress with the steady rhythm of determination.

Together, we embark on this transformative journey where problem-solving is the linchpin of goal achievement. As we set our sights on personal development, career success, and mental well-being, may we find in problem-solving not just a skill but a faithful companion that paves the way to the realization of our most cherished aspirations.

Emotional Regulation: In the tapestry of our emotional lives, problem-solving emerges as the master weaver, crafting a fabric of rationality amidst the intricate threads of our feelings. It is this rational mindset, nurtured by problem-solving, that becomes our guardian against the storm of overwhelming emotions.

Challenges and setbacks often stir the tempestuous seas of our emotions. However, problem solvers approach these emotional squalls with a steadfast determination to uncover solutions. This rational perspective acts as a buoy, keeping them afloat amid the tumultuous waters, preventing them from being swallowed by the depths of negative emotions.

Emotional stability, born from the crucible of problem-solving, becomes the bedrock of mental well-being. It is the ability to navigate the swells of emotions with grace and composure, to find equilibrium in the face of adversity. This emotional regulation is not about suppressing emotions but about understanding and managing them in a healthy, constructive way.

Together, we embark on this profound journey where problem-solving becomes the beacon of emotional regulation. As we confront life's challenges with a rational mindset, may we discover the harmony that lies within emotional stability, ensuring that our mental well-being remains resilient and unwavering in the face of life's emotional tempests.

Conflict Resolution: In the intricate web of human interactions, conflicts are the knots that often appear. Yet, within the art of problem-solving lies the wisdom to untangle these knots, to transform conflicts into bridges of understanding. Effective problem solvers possess a unique skill—they are the architects of peace.

When problems involve conflicts with others, problem solvers approach these situations with the precision of diplomats. They are skilled navigators of disagreement, able to traverse the tumultuous waters of differing perspectives and find common ground on which understanding can flourish. Through this process, they not only resolve conflicts but also strengthen relationships.

Conflict resolution becomes the cornerstone of maintaining mental well-being and fostering healthy interactions with others. It is the art of dismantling barriers to harmony and replacing them with bridges of empathy. As individuals learn to navigate conflicts with grace and wisdom, they not only preserve their own mental well-being but also contribute to a more peaceful and cooperative world.

Together, we embark on this transformative journey where problem-solving is the catalyst for conflict resolution. As we navigate the complexities of human relationships, may we discover that conflicts are not insurmountable obstacles but opportunities for greater understanding and stronger connections, ultimately leading to mental well-being and harmonious interactions with others.

Continuous Learning: Within the realm of problem-solving lies a profound truth—it is a journey of perpetual learning. Each problem, like an unopened book, holds the promise of new insights, skills, and knowledge. Through the act of problem-solving, we become lifelong learners, and this continuous learning is the fertile soil for personal growth and mental well-being.

Problem-solving, in its essence, is not just about finding solutions; it is about the process of discovery. It is the unwrapping of life's mysteries, one challenge at a time. As we engage with problems, we cultivate a growth mindset, a mindset that sees in each challenge an opportunity for growth and learning.

The pursuit of continuous learning is not a mere academic endeavor; it is a path to self-improvement and enriched mental well-being. It fosters a sense of curiosity—an insatiable desire to understand the world around us and the inner workings of our own minds. It is through this curiosity that we remain open to new experiences and possibilities.

Together, we embark on this transformative journey where problem-solving becomes the gateway to continuous learning. As we confront life's challenges, may we do so with the heart of a student, eager to unravel the mysteries that lie before us. Through the lens of problem-solving, may we cultivate a lifelong love for learning, ensuring that our journey is not just one of growth, but of boundless curiosity and self-discovery.

In "Mastering Problem-Solving for Enhanced Mental Health and Personal Growth," problem-solving skills are not just a means to overcome obstacles; they are a pathway to self-discovery and empowerment. By honing these skills, readers can build resilience, reduce stress, and unlock their potential for personal growth and mental well-being, ultimately leading to a more fulfilling and empowered life.

Developing problem-solving skills

Developing problem-solving skills is a valuable asset in various aspects of life, from personal challenges to professional endeavors. Here are the steps to help you enhance your problem-solving abilities:

Identify the Problem:

- Clearly define the problem you are facing. Make sure you understand its nature, scope, and any constraints involved.

Gather Information:

- Collect relevant data and information about the problem. This may involve research, data analysis, or consulting experts.

Generate Alternative Solutions:

- Brainstorm a variety of potential solutions or approaches to address the problem. Encourage creativity and consider both conventional and unconventional options.

Evaluate Each Solution:

- Assess the pros and cons of each solution. Consider factors such as feasibility, cost, time, and potential risks. This step may require further research or analysis.

Choose the Best Solution:

- Select the solution that appears to be the most effective and practical. It should align with your goals and the resources available.

Develop an Action Plan:

- Create a detailed plan outlining the steps required to implement your chosen solution. This plan should include timelines, responsibilities, and milestones.

Implement the Solution:

- Put your action plan into action. Execute the steps you've outlined, and monitor progress as you work towards solving the problem.

Adapt and Adjust:

- Be flexible and open to modifications if necessary. Sometimes, unexpected challenges arise during implementation, and you may need to adjust your approach.

Evaluate the Outcome:

- Assess the results of your problem-solving efforts. Did your solution effectively address the problem? What lessons can you learn from the process?

Learn and Iterate:

- Reflect on the entire problem-solving process. Identify what worked well and what could be improved. Use this feedback to enhance your problem-solving skills for future challenges.

Seek Feedback:

- Don't hesitate to seek feedback from others, especially if the problem-solving process involves a team or group. Different perspectives can provide valuable insights.

Practice Regularly:

- Problem-solving skills improve with practice. Seek out opportunities to tackle new challenges, even if they are relatively small, to hone your abilities.

Stay Curious and Inquisitive:

- Cultivate a mindset of curiosity. Ask questions, explore alternatives, and remain open to learning. This mindset can help you identify problems and solutions more effectively.

Develop Critical Thinking Skills:

- Critical thinking involves analyzing information, identifying patterns, and making sound judgments. Strengthening your critical thinking abilities can significantly enhance your problem-solving skills.

Embrace Failure as a Learning Opportunity:

- Understand that not every problem-solving attempt will be successful. When you encounter setbacks, view them as opportunities to learn and grow.

Seek Guidance:

- Don't hesitate to seek guidance or mentorship from individuals who excel in problem-solving. Learning from others' experiences can be invaluable.

Remember that problem-solving is a skill that improves over time with practice and continuous learning. By following these steps and being persistent in your efforts, you can become a more effective problem solver in various aspects of your life.

"The only person you are destined to become is the person you decide to be."

— Ralph Waldo Emerson

Chapter 1: The Foundation of Resilience: Understanding Problem-Solving

Section 1: The Essence of Resilience

In this opening chapter, we embark on a journey into the heart of resilience and lay the groundwork for unleashing our inner strength.

Resilience is not merely the ability to withstand adversity but the capacity to thrive despite it. It's a quality that enables us to adapt, grow, and flourish even in the face of life's most formidable challenges.

Step 1: Defining Resilience

Resilience, a term often mentioned but not always fully understood, serves as the cornerstone of our journey through the intricate realms of problem-solving, personal growth, and mental well-being. In this chapter, we embark on a quest to define resilience, unraveling its multifaceted nature and uncovering its profound significance in our lives.

The Art of Bouncing Back

At its core, resilience is the art of bouncing back and weathering the storms of life with courage and determination. It is the ability to withstand adversity, to bend without breaking, and to emerge from challenges stronger and wiser than before. Resilience is not merely about surviving; it's about thriving in the face of adversity.

Emotional, Mental, and Physical Fortitude

Resilience is a comprehensive concept that extends its embrace to every facet of our being. It encompasses emotional resilience, enabling us to manage and recover from emotional upheavals. It embodies mental resilience, equipping us with the cognitive and psychological tools to navigate complex problems and setbacks. Moreover, it embodies physical resilience, enhancing our physical health and vitality, which in turn bolsters our mental well-being.

Stories, Anecdotes, and Scientific Insights

Throughout this exploration, we will weave a tapestry of understanding using a variety of threads. We'll share inspiring stories of individuals who have demonstrated remarkable resilience in the face of seemingly insurmountable challenges. Anecdotes from real-life experiences will offer practical glimpses into how resilience manifests in everyday life. And, underpinning it all, we'll delve into scientific insights from psychology, neuroscience, and related disciplines to uncover the mechanisms that enable resilience to flourish.

Stories of Resilience

The Phoenix Rises: Sarah, a single mother, faced financial hardship and personal loss in quick succession. Despite the odds, she not only managed to provide for her family but also pursued her passion for painting. Through her art, she found solace and a newfound sense of purpose, embodying the resilience that can arise from adversity.

From Paralysis to Paralympics: Mark, a professional athlete, suffered a life-altering spinal cord injury. Instead of succumbing to despair, he embarked on a grueling rehabilitation journey. With unwavering determination, he not only regained his physical abilities but also competed in the Paralympic Games, showcasing the incredible resilience of the human spirit.

Anecdotes of Everyday Resilience

The Daily Commute: Maria, a city dweller, navigates the chaotic rush hour traffic daily. Despite the stress and frustration, she practices mindfulness techniques during her commute, turning a daily struggle into an opportunity for mental resilience and personal growth.

The Unexpected Job Loss: John unexpectedly lost his job, sending his life into turmoil. Instead of dwelling on the setback, he immediately began networking, enhancing his skills, and exploring new career opportunities. His proactive response illustrates how resilience can transform unexpected setbacks into stepping stones.

Scientific Insights into Resilience

Neuroplasticity and Resilience: Research in neuroscience has revealed the brain's remarkable ability to adapt and rewire itself, a phenomenon known as neuroplasticity. This insight suggests that we can develop resilience by consciously rewiring our thought patterns and responses to adversity.

The Role of Social Support: Studies in psychology emphasize the pivotal role of social support in building resilience. Strong social connections provide emotional buoyancy during difficult times and are a key factor in enhancing mental well-being.

Stress Hormones and Resilience: Scientific research shows that our bodies release stress hormones during challenging situations. Over time, with proper coping mechanisms, our bodies can become more resilient to the physical effects of stress, contributing to overall health and well-being.

These stories, anecdotes, and scientific insights serve as the building blocks of our exploration into resilience. They illustrate the real-world applications and the profound impact that understanding and harnessing resilience can have on our personal growth and mental well-being. In the chapters ahead, we will delve deeper into practical strategies for cultivating and strengthening resilience, equipping you with the tools to navigate life's challenges with grace and fortitude.

Why Resilience Matters

Understanding resilience is not an academic exercise; it's an essential journey for anyone seeking personal growth and mental well-being. Resilience equips us with the tools to confront life's obstacles head-on, fostering a sense of agency and empowerment. It is the key to not only surviving but thriving in the ever-changing landscapes of our lives.

In the chapters to come, we will explore how resilience can be cultivated, strengthened, and applied to the art of problem-solving. By mastering resilience, you will not only bounce back from adversity but use it as a springboard for personal growth and well-being. Together, we will unlock the secrets to becoming more resilient individuals, ready to face life's challenges with unwavering strength and optimism.

Step 2: The Resilient Mindset

Resilience starts with the mind—a mindset that refuses to be defeated. In this step, we'll explore the characteristics of a resilient mindset. We'll delve into the power of optimism, the importance of adaptability, and the role of self-belief. By understanding the building blocks of a resilient mindset, we'll begin to lay the foundation for our own transformation.

At the heart of resilience lies a powerful force—the resilient mindset. This mindset is the bedrock upon which the ability to bounce back from adversity is built. In this section, we'll embark on a journey to understand the key characteristics that define a resilient mindset, exploring the formidable power of optimism, the flexibility of adaptability, and the unwavering strength of self-belief. As we delve into these building blocks of resilience, we'll set the stage for our personal transformation.

Optimism: The Fuel of Resilience

Optimism is the wellspring of resilience—a mindset that refuses to surrender to despair. It's the unwavering belief that even in the darkest of moments, there's a glimmer of hope, an opportunity for growth. Optimism isn't about denying the existence of problems; it's about acknowledging them while maintaining faith in your ability to overcome them.

Adaptability: Embracing Change

The resilient mindset thrives on adaptability. It recognizes that life is a dynamic, ever-evolving journey, and the ability to adapt to changing circumstances is paramount. Rather than resisting change, a resilient mindset sees it as a chance for growth, a new adventure waiting to unfold.

Self-Belief: The Rock of Resilience

Perhaps the most crucial element of a resilient mindset is self-belief. It's the inner conviction that you possess the strength and capabilities to navigate life's challenges. Self-belief empowers you to take action, to persevere when faced with adversity, and to tap into your reservoirs of inner strength.

Building the Foundation for Transformation

As we explore the characteristics of a resilient mindset, remember that these traits are not fixed; they can be cultivated and strengthened. Through the stories, anecdotes, and scientific insights we've discussed, you've already glimpsed the transformative power of resilience. Now, it's time to apply these principles to your own life.

In the chapters ahead, we'll delve deeper into practical strategies and exercises designed to nurture your resilient mindset. By embracing optimism, cultivating adaptability, and fortifying your self-belief, you'll be equipped to not only weather life's storms but to use them as catalysts for personal growth and mental well-being. Your journey toward mastering problem-solving, enhancing your resilience, and fostering personal growth has just begun, and the resilient mindset is your compass guiding you towards a brighter, more resilient future.

Section 2: The Role of Problem-Solving

Step 3: The Problem-Solving Connection

Resilience and problem-solving are inseparable companions on our journey. In this step, we'll unravel the profound connection between resilience and problem-solving. We'll explore how effective problem-solving is not just a tool for overcoming obstacles but the very essence of resilience itself. Through real-life examples, we'll see how individuals have harnessed problem-solving skills to emerge from adversity stronger than ever.

In our exploration of resilience and its profound impact on personal growth and mental well-being, we now arrive at a critical juncture: the inseparable connection between resilience and problem-solving. These two concepts are not mere companions; they are intertwined in a dynamic and symbiotic relationship. In this step, we'll delve into the intricacies of this connection, revealing that effective problem-solving is not just a tool for overcoming obstacles; it is, in fact, the very essence of resilience itself.

Problem-Solving: The Heart of Resilience

Imagine resilience as a mighty tree with problem-solving at its core, much like a sturdy trunk. Just as a tree's roots anchor it firmly to the ground, problem-solving serves as the anchor for resilience, grounding it in practical action. Resilience is not passive; it is an active force, and problem-solving is the means by which it propels us forward.

The Path of Problem-Solving Resilience

To illustrate this concept, we turn to real-life examples of individuals who have harnessed problem-solving skills to emerge from adversity stronger than ever:

The Entrepreneurial Triumph: Sarah, a budding entrepreneur, who faced a series of setbacks when launching her business startup. Instead of succumbing to failure, she embraced these challenges as opportunities to refine her business model, adapt to market demands, and ultimately, achieve unprecedented success. Her story showcases how problem-solving resilience can transform obstacles into stepping stones.

From Grief to Growth: John, grieving the loss of a loved one, found solace and healing through creative expression. He channeled his emotions into writing and art, using problem-solving skills to navigate his grief constructively. In doing so, he not only found personal growth but also discovered the therapeutic power of problem-solving as a tool for emotional resilience.

Unlocking the Power of Problem-Solving Resilience

As we delve deeper into the relationship between resilience and problem-solving, it becomes evident that mastering problem-solving is not only a valuable skill but a fundamental aspect of our capacity to bounce back from adversity. By honing our problem-solving skills, we become better equipped to navigate life's challenges, transforming them into opportunities for growth and personal development.

In the upcoming chapters, we will explore practical techniques and strategies for enhancing your problem-solving resilience. You will learn to view problems not as insurmountable obstacles but as puzzles waiting to be solved. By embracing this mindset and developing your problem-solving prowess, you will harness the full potential of resilience, paving the way for personal growth and a resilient, flourishing life.

Step 4: Problem-Solving as a Skill

Problem-solving isn't a mystical gift bestowed upon a fortunate few; it's a skill that can be honed and mastered. In this step, we'll dissect problem-solving into its core components—identifying problems, analyzing them, generating solutions, and implementing those solutions. We'll discover that these skills are not exclusive to a select group but are accessible to all, waiting to be cultivated.

The notion of problem-solving often carries an air of mystique, as if it were a rare gift granted to a select few. However, in this step, we will unravel the myth surrounding problem-solving, revealing it as a skill that can be honed and mastered by anyone. By dissecting problem-solving into its core components—identifying problems, analyzing them, generating solutions, and implementing those solutions—we will unveil the practical and accessible nature of these skills.

Demystifying Problem-Solving

Problem-solving, at its essence, is a structured process that can be learned, practiced, and refined. It is not the exclusive domain of geniuses or experts; rather, it is a fundamental human ability waiting to be cultivated. The journey to becoming an adept problem solver begins with understanding the components that make up this skill.

The Four Pillars of Problem-Solving

Identifying Problems: The first step in effective problem-solving is recognizing the existence of a problem. It involves honing your ability to perceive challenges, whether they are overt obstacles or subtle nuances in your life. Sharpening your problem recognition skills allows you to address issues before they escalate.

Analyzing Problems: Once a problem is identified, the next step is to analyze it thoroughly. This entails breaking down complex issues into manageable parts, understanding the underlying causes, and considering their implications. Analytical thinking is the cornerstone of effective problem-solving.

Generating Solutions: Problem-solving extends beyond analysis; it demands creativity in generating potential solutions. This phase encourages you to think broadly and inventively, exploring a range of possibilities before settling on a course of action. It's a stage where innovation and lateral thinking flourish.

Implementing Solutions: Identifying problems, analyzing them, and generating solutions are meaningful only when those solutions are put into action. Effective implementation requires planning, commitment, and adaptability, as well as the capacity to learn from successes and setbacks.

Cultivating Your Problem-Solving Skills

As you progress through this journey, remember that problem-solving is not a static skill but a dynamic one that evolves with practice. By understanding these four pillars of problem-solving, you'll be better equipped to approach challenges in your life with confidence and resilience.

In the forthcoming chapters, we will explore practical exercises and techniques designed to strengthen each of these problem-solving components. As you hone your problem-solving skills, you'll not only become a more adept solver of life's puzzles but also enhance your capacity for personal growth and mental well-being. Problem-solving is not a mystery; it's a skill within your grasp, waiting to be cultivated and mastered.

Section 3: Problem-Solving for Resilience

Resilience refers to the capacity of individuals, communities, or systems to adapt, bounce back, and recover from adversity, challenges, or setbacks. It is the ability to withstand and navigate through difficult circumstances, stressors, or traumatic events while maintaining mental well-being and overall functioning. Resilience involves not only the process of overcoming difficulties but also the development of personal strength and the capability to thrive despite adverse conditions.

Key aspects of resilience include:

Adaptability: Resilient individuals can adjust and adapt to changing circumstances, finding effective ways to cope with challenges.

Emotional Regulation: Resilience involves the ability to manage and regulate emotions, maintaining a balanced and positive outlook even in challenging situations.

Positive Coping Strategies: Resilient people often employ constructive coping mechanisms, such as problem-solving, seeking support, and maintaining a sense of optimism.

Social Support: Having a supportive network of friends, family, or community is crucial for resilience. Strong social connections can provide emotional support and resources during difficult times.

Self-Efficacy: Resilient individuals possess a belief in their own abilities and a sense of control over their lives, contributing to a proactive approach in facing challenges.

Learning and Growth: Resilience involves a process of learning and growth through adversity, where individuals can emerge stronger, wiser, and more resourceful.

Resilience is not a fixed trait but rather a dynamic quality that can be developed and strengthened over time. It is influenced by a combination of personal characteristics, life experiences, and external support systems. Building resilience often involves cultivating a positive mindset, developing coping skills, fostering social connections, and learning from challenging experiences.

Step 5: Problem-Solving as Resilience Builder

Now that we understand the building blocks of resilience and problem-solving, we'll explore how these skills intersect. Problem-solving becomes a vehicle for resilience as we learn to approach life's challenges with a solution-oriented mindset. We'll see how problem-solving empowers us to face adversity head-on, navigate obstacles with grace, and emerge from setbacks even more resilient than before.

Having dissected the components of both resilience and problem-solving, we now arrive at a pivotal juncture where these two powerful concepts intersect. Problem-solving, when viewed through the lens of resilience, becomes a potent vehicle for personal growth and mental well-being. In this step, we will explore how problem-solving serves as a builder of resilience, equipping us to approach life's challenges with a solution-oriented mindset. Through this perspective, we will come to understand how problem-solving empowers us to confront adversity head-on, navigate obstacles with grace, and emerge from setbacks even more resilient than before.

The Resilience-Problem-Solving Nexus

Imagine resilience and problem-solving as two gears in a well-oiled machine, working in perfect harmony. When challenges arise, these gears begin to turn, channeling adversity into opportunity. Problem-solving becomes the means by which resilience is put into action, while resilience, in turn, strengthens our resolve to confront problems.

Problem-Solving as an Active Resilience Builder

Consider this scenario: You encounter a significant setback in your career. Rather than succumbing to despair, your resilient mindset engages problem-solving mode. You identify the root causes of the setback, analyze potential solutions, and develop a strategic plan for recovery. As you implement this plan, you not only resolve the issue but also emerge from it with newfound knowledge, confidence, and resilience. In this way, problem-solving acts as an active builder of resilience.

Facing Adversity Head-On

One of the most remarkable attributes of problem-solving as a resilience builder is its capacity to enable us to face adversity head-on. Rather than retreating or becoming overwhelmed by challenges, we approach them with a sense of agency and optimism. We see problems not as insurmountable barriers but as opportunities for growth and transformation.

Navigating Obstacles with Grace

Problem-solving equips us with the tools to navigate life's obstacles with grace and poise. We become adept at managing stress, making effective decisions, and adapting to changing circumstances. These skills are not only essential for solving immediate problems but are also invaluable for building long-term resilience.

Emerging Stronger Than Before

Perhaps the most inspiring aspect of problem-solving as a resilience builder is its capacity to help us emerge from setbacks even stronger than before. Each problem we solve becomes a stepping stone on our journey of personal growth and mental well-being. With each challenge overcome, we accumulate a wealth of experience and wisdom that fortifies our resilience for the future.

The Resilience-Problem-Solving Cycle

As we conclude this step, it's important to recognize that resilience and problem-solving do not exist in isolation; they form a continuous cycle. The resilience gained from successfully addressing one challenge enhances our problem-solving abilities, enabling us to tackle the next challenge with even greater efficacy. This synergy between resilience and problem-solving is a powerful force, one that can lead us to a life characterized by growth, adaptability, and unwavering strength.

In the chapters ahead, we will delve into practical techniques and exercises that will further integrate problem-solving into your resilience-building toolkit. By embracing this synergy, you'll be better equipped to not only weather life's storms but to use them as catalysts for personal growth and a life rich in resilience.

Step 6: Developing Problem-Solving Skills

In this step, we roll up our sleeves and begin the journey of developing effective problem-solving skills. We'll explore practical strategies for enhancing our problem-solving abilities, from improving decision-making to fostering creativity in finding solutions. This step is a hands-on workshop, equipping us with the tools we need for the road ahead.

With a solid understanding of the resilience-problem-solving connection, we are now ready to roll up our sleeves and embark on the journey of developing effective problem-solving skills. In this step, we will delve into the practical strategies and techniques that will enable us to enhance our problem-solving abilities. From improving decision-making to fostering creativity in finding solutions, this step serves as a hands-on workshop, equipping us with the essential tools needed for the road ahead.

Sharpening Decision-Making Skills

Effective problem-solving often hinges on making sound decisions. To enhance your decision-making skills:

Gather Information: Begin by collecting relevant information about the problem at hand. The more data you have, the better-informed your decisions will be.

Consider Alternatives: Generate a range of potential solutions. Avoid settling for the first option that comes to mind; explore various alternatives, no matter how unconventional they may seem.

Evaluate Pros and Cons: Assess the advantages and disadvantages of each solution. This process will help you make a well-informed decision based on a thorough analysis.

Seek Input: Don't hesitate to seek input from others. Collaborative decision-making often leads to more robust solutions.

Trust Your Instincts: While data and input are valuable, also trust your instincts and intuition. Sometimes, a gut feeling can lead to innovative solutions.

Fostering Creativity in Problem-Solving

Creativity is a key element of effective problem-solving. To cultivate creativity in finding solutions:

Divergent Thinking: Encourage divergent thinking, which involves generating multiple ideas, even if they initially seem unrelated or unconventional.

Brainstorming: Engage in brainstorming sessions with others to explore a wide range of ideas and perspectives.

Mindfulness and Relaxation: Practice mindfulness and relaxation techniques to reduce stress and mental clutter, allowing creative ideas to surface.

Embrace Failure: Understand that failure is often a part of the creative process. Don't be discouraged by setbacks; view them as opportunities to learn and innovate.

Practical Problem-Solving Exercises

To put your developing problem-solving skills into practice:

Real-Life Scenarios: Identify real-life problems or challenges you're currently facing. Apply the decision-making and creativity techniques to find solutions.

Role-Playing: Engage in role-playing exercises with friends or colleagues, simulating problem-solving scenarios to refine your skills.

Case Studies: Study case examples of successful problem-solving in various fields. Analyze how individuals or teams tackled complex issues and what strategies they employed.

Journaling: Keep a problem-solving journal to record your experiences, challenges, and solutions. Reflect on what worked and what could be improved.

Remember that developing problem-solving skills is an ongoing journey. Like any skill, it requires practice and persistence. As you work through this step, embrace the process of growth and learning. With each problem you solve and each decision you make, you are not only honing your problem-solving abilities but also strengthening your resilience. The journey of mastery is a rewarding one, and as you continue, you'll find that problem-solving becomes an integral part of your approach to life's challenges, enhancing your overall well-being and personal growth.

Step 7: The Power of Perspective

Lastly, we'll uncover the transformative power of perspective in problem-solving. The lens through which we view challenges can either hinder or enhance our resilience. By shifting our perspective, we can turn obstacles into opportunities and setbacks into stepping stones. We'll learn to embrace the idea that every problem we encounter is a chance for growth.

In our final step, we turn our attention to a truly transformative aspect of problem-solving—perspective. The lens through which we view challenges can either hinder or enhance our resilience. By shifting our perspective, we can turn obstacles into opportunities and setbacks into stepping stones. In this step, we'll explore the profound notion that every problem we encounter is a chance for growth.

The Lens We Choose

Our perspective shapes our reality. When we encounter a problem, we can choose to view it through a lens of defeat and despair or through one of optimism and opportunity. The lens we choose has a profound impact on our resilience and our ability to solve problems effectively.

Obstacles as Opportunities

Embracing a perspective that views obstacles as opportunities allows us to approach problems with curiosity and open-mindedness. Instead of fearing challenges, we welcome them as chances to learn, grow, and evolve. This perspective fuels our resilience, driving us to tackle problems head-on.

Setbacks as Stepping Stones

Similarly, setbacks need not be seen as failures; they can be stepping stones on our journey to success. When we encounter setbacks, we have an opportunity to reflect, adapt, and refine our approach. Each setback brings us one step closer to our goals, provided we view it as a valuable lesson rather than a defeat.

Growth Through Every Problem

Ultimately, the power of perspective lies in recognizing that every problem we encounter, no matter how big or small, offers the potential for growth. Whether it's a personal challenge, a professional obstacle, or a societal issue, each problem can serve as a catalyst for positive change.

Practical Perspective-Shifting Techniques

To harness the power of perspective in problem-solving:

Reframe Negative Thoughts: When negative thoughts arise in the face of a problem, consciously reframe them in a more positive light. For example, instead of thinking, "I can't do this," shift your perspective to, "This is a chance to learn something new."

Practice Gratitude: Cultivate a habit of gratitude by regularly acknowledging the positive aspects of your life, even in the midst of challenges. This can help shift your perspective towards a more optimistic outlook.

Seek Diverse Input: Engage with people who have different perspectives and experiences. Their insights can broaden your own perspective and offer new solutions to problems.

Embracing the Journey of Growth

As we conclude our journey of problem-solving for resilience, remember that the power of perspective is an ever-present tool in your toolkit. By choosing to view challenges as opportunities and setbacks as stepping stones, you not only enhance your resilience but also enrich your life with continuous growth and personal development.

Each problem you encounter is a chance to learn, adapt, and thrive. As you continue on your path, may you approach each challenge with a perspective that fuels your resilience and propels you toward a future filled with opportunities and possibilities.

As we conclude Chapter 1, we'll have laid a solid foundation for our journey. We'll understand the essence of resilience, the importance of a resilient mindset, and the pivotal role that problem-solving plays in our quest for personal growth and mental well-being. Now, armed with this knowledge, we're prepared to delve deeper into the art of problem-solving and discover how it can unlock our inner resilience.

Chapter 2: Navigating Life's Labyrinth: The Problem-Solving Mindset

"The Enchanted Labyrinth of Wisdom"

In a quaint village nestled between rolling hills and a winding river, there lived a young girl named Elara. She was known for her insatiable curiosity and her unwavering determination. But there was one quality that set her apart from everyone else—her remarkable problem-solving skills.

One sunny morning, as Elara was exploring the forest near her village, she stumbled upon a peculiar-looking stone. It was not just any stone; it had an intricate carving of a key on its surface. Intrigued, Elara decided to follow the trail of similar stones that led her deeper into the forest.

As she ventured farther, the forest began to change. The trees grew taller and more ancient, and the air was filled with a sense of mystery. It wasn't long before she realized she had entered an enchanted labyrinth, a place known only to a few who dared to explore it.

In the heart of the labyrinth, Elara came across a massive oak tree, its branches forming a natural canopy that seemed to shield a hidden secret. Under the tree's majestic roots, she found a treasure chest, sealed with a lock that bore the same key she had seen on the stone. This was the moment when her problem-solving skills would be put to the test.

With determination in her heart, Elara began to solve the intricate puzzle that guarded the chest. She knew that every twist and turn of the puzzle held a clue—a lesson in problem-solving that the enchanted labyrinth had prepared for her. With each challenge she faced, her skills grew sharper and her mind became more agile.

Finally, after hours of careful consideration and unwavering determination, Elara unlocked the chest. Inside, she found a scroll, aged with time, containing wisdom that had been hidden for generations. It was a testament to her ability to solve complex problems, to persevere in the face of adversity, and to embrace the joy of discovery.

As Elara emerged from the enchanted labyrinth, her heart brimming with newfound knowledge and wisdom, she realized that the journey itself had been the greatest treasure. The lessons she had learned along the way, the challenges she had overcome, and the growth she had experienced had transformed her into a problem-solving virtuoso.

Elara returned to her village, not as a young girl but as a problem-solving sage. She shared her tale of the enchanted labyrinth, inspiring others to cultivate a problem-solving mindset within themselves. The village soon became a haven for those seeking to embrace challenges with open arms, to view problems as opportunities, and to embark on a journey of continuous learning.

And so, in the heart of the village, they erected a statue of Elara, holding the key to the enchanted labyrinth. It served as a reminder that the greatest treasures in life are often hidden behind the doors of problems, waiting for those who possess the problem-solving mindset to unlock them and embark on a journey of wisdom and growth.

Section 1: Cultivating the Problem-Solving Mindset

Step 1: The Power of Positive Thinking

Welcome to the first chapter of our exploration into the problem-solving mindset—a mindset that serves as the bedrock of our ability to confront challenges, nurture resilience, and embark on a path towards personal growth and mental well-being. In this initial step, we will dive into the transformative power of positive thinking, a cornerstone of the problem-solving mindset.

Positive Thinking: A Catalyst for Problem-Solving

Positive thinking is more than a simple cliché; it is a potent force that shapes our perception of the world and, in turn, our responses to it. At its core, positive thinking is about adopting an optimistic outlook, even in the face of adversity. It involves reframing challenges as opportunities and setbacks as stepping stones towards growth.

The Resilience-Positive Thinking Connection

Consider resilience and positive thinking as intertwined threads in the fabric of your mindset. When challenges arise, positive thinking fuels your resilience, enabling you to approach problems with unwavering determination and creativity. It serves as a mental toolkit, empowering you to navigate life's labyrinth with a sense of hope and possibility.

Practical Steps Toward Positive Thinking

Mindfulness and Self-Awareness: Start by becoming more aware of your thoughts and emotions. Mindfulness practices can help you observe your thinking patterns and identify negative thought loops.

Reframing Negative Thoughts: When negative thoughts arise, consciously challenge and reframe them. For example, instead of thinking, "I can't do this," shift your perspective to, "I may face challenges, but I have the ability to overcome them."

Gratitude Journaling: It is recommendable that you dedicate time each day to reflect on the positive aspects of your life. Write down things you are grateful for, no matter how small. This practice will help you cultivate a more optimistic mindset.

Surround Yourself with Positivity: Seek out people, books, and resources that inspire and uplift you. Positive influences in your environment can reinforce your commitment to positive thinking.

Visualization: Practice visualizing successful outcomes when faced with challenges. This mental rehearsal can boost your confidence and problem-solving abilities.

Embracing the Power of Positive Thinking

As you embark on this journey to cultivate a problem-solving mindset, remember that positive thinking is not about denying the existence of problems or ignoring difficulties. It's about approaching them with a belief in your ability to overcome them, to learn from them, and to emerge from them stronger and wiser.

In the chapters ahead, we will continue to explore how positive thinking intertwines with problem-solving and resilience. By adopting this mindset, you'll not only enhance your capacity to solve problems effectively but also nurture a sense of empowerment, well-being, and personal growth that will enrich every aspect of your life.

Step 2: Embracing Change and Adaptation

Change, as the saying goes, is the only constant in life. As we navigate the intricate labyrinth of our existence, we encounter change at every turn. In this step, we will delve into the role of adaptability within the problem-solving mindset. Effective problem solvers are not resistant to change; instead, they embrace it as an opportunity for growth.

Through stories of adaptability in the face of adversity, we will uncover the power of flexibility in problem-solving.

The Dynamic Nature of Life

Life is inherently dynamic, and the ability to adapt to changing circumstances is a hallmark of resilience and problem-solving prowess. When we view change not as a disruption but as a natural part of our journey, we unlock new avenues for growth and innovation.

Adaptability: The Bridge to Resilience

Think of adaptability as the bridge connecting problem-solving and resilience. When we encounter change, whether in our personal lives or professional endeavors, our adaptability is tested. Those who possess a strong problem-solving mindset approach change as an opportunity to apply their skills and navigate new challenges.

Stories of Adaptability

Let's explore a few stories that illustrate the transformative power of adaptability in problem-solving:

The Career Pivot: Sarah, a corporate executive, faced a significant career change due to industry shifts. Instead of resisting this change, she embraced it as an opportunity to explore her passion for a different field. Her adaptability not only led to a successful career transition but also enriched her life in unexpected ways.

From Student to Entrepreneur: John, a recent college graduate, experienced an uncertain job market upon graduation. Rather than waiting for a traditional job offer, he adapted by launching his own startup. His entrepreneurial journey not only provided employment but also showcased how adaptability can turn adversity into innovation.

Practical Steps Towards Adaptability

Develop a Growth Mindset: Embrace the belief that you can develop and grow through challenges and change. This mindset fosters adaptability by encouraging continuous learning and improvement.

Practice Flexibility: Cultivate the ability to pivot when necessary. Be open to exploring new strategies, ideas, and approaches when faced with change.

Seek Learning Opportunities: View change as an opportunity to acquire new skills and knowledge. Seek out courses, books, or mentors that can help you adapt effectively.

Embrace Resilience-Building Practices: Incorporate stress management techniques, mindfulness, and self-care into your daily routine. These practices can enhance your emotional resilience and adaptability.

The Power of Adaptability in Problem-Solving

As you embark on the journey of embracing change and adaptation within the problem-solving mindset, remember that adaptability is not a sign of weakness but a testament to your resilience and growth. By embracing change as an opportunity, you'll not only become a more effective problem solver but also cultivate a sense of empowerment and adaptability that will serve you well in the face of life's ever-evolving landscape. In the chapters that follow, we will continue to explore how adaptability, resilience, and problem-solving intertwine, forging a path towards personal growth and unwavering strength.

Section 2: The Creative Problem-Solving Process

Step 3: Identifying Problems with Clarity

In the journey of effective problem-solving, the crucial first step is gaining a clear understanding of the issues we face. In this step, we will immerse ourselves in the art of problem identification. By distinguishing between symptoms and root causes, we can tackle problems at their source. Through practical exercises and real-world examples, we will sharpen our problem-recognition skills.

The Importance of Problem Identification

Imagine a medical doctor faced with a patient presenting various symptoms. Effective treatment can only begin when the doctor accurately identifies the underlying ailment. Similarly, in problem-solving, we must discern the true nature of the challenge before applying solutions. Problem identification is the gateway to effective problem-solving.

Symptoms vs. Root Causes

Problems often manifest as symptoms—visible signs of an underlying issue. To identify problems with clarity, we must differentiate between these symptoms and the root causes. Symptoms are the surface-level indications, while root causes are the deeper, often hidden, sources of the problem.

Sharpening Problem-Recognition Skills

To enhance your ability to identify problems effectively you must:

Ask "Why?" Repeatedly: Utilize the "Five Whys" technique. When you encounter a problem, ask "Why is this happening?" Then, ask "Why" again in response to the previous answer. Continue this process until you uncover the root cause.

Gather Information: Seek as much information as possible about the problem. Talk to those affected, research related issues, and collect data to gain a comprehensive understanding.

Analyze Patterns: Look for patterns or recurring themes in the problems you encounter. These patterns can often lead you to the underlying root causes.

The "Seven Key Steps to Solve a Problem" provide a structured approach to effective problem-solving. Let's delve into each step in detail:

1. Define the Problem:

• Be Clear and 'SMART': Clearly articulate the problem using Specific, Measurable, Achievable, Relevant, and Time-bound criteria.

• Be Objective: Approach the problem without biases and emotions, focusing on facts and observable behaviors.

• Focus on Maintenance: Identify what perpetuates the problem rather than its root causes.

- Set Realistic Goals: Establish achievable objectives for resolving the problem.

2. Generate Potential Solutions:

- Brainstorm: Encourage a free-flowing generation of ideas without judgment.

- Eliminate Infeasible Solutions: Remove options that are illegal, unethical, or unreasonable after brainstorming.

- List Preferred Solutions: Based on goals, prioritize and list the most viable solutions.

3. Evaluate Alternatives:

- Decision Making: Assess challenges and benefits for the top 3 or 4 solutions.

- Consider Multiple Views: Gather diverse perspectives to broaden the evaluation.

4. Decide on a Solution:

- Choose 1 or 2 Solutions: Make a decision based on the evaluation.

- Specify Actions: Clearly define the steps or actions required to implement the chosen solution.

- Assign Responsibilities: Indicate who will be responsible for each action.

- Specify Implementation Details: Clearly outline how and when the action will be executed.

5. Implement Solution:

- Plan Execution: Develop a detailed plan for carrying out the chosen solution.

- Implementation: Execute the solution as planned.

6. Evaluate the Outcome:

- Assess Effectiveness: Evaluate how well the solution addressed the problem.

- Consider Revisions: Decide if the current plan needs revision, if better skills are required, or if skills can be used more effectively.

7. Review What Happened:

- Identify Barriers: Explore obstacles that may have hindered effective problem-solving.

- Examine Attitude/Emotion: Consider the impact of negative attitudes or emotions.

- Reflect on Problem-Solving Style: Evaluate your preferred style of problem-solving.

- Manage Emotion: Be mindful of emotional influences during the problem-solving process.

- Examine Thoughts and Beliefs: Reflect on how thoughts and beliefs may have influenced the problem-solving approach.

- Consider Other Problems: Acknowledge additional problems that may need attention.

By following these seven key steps and addressing potential barriers, individuals can enhance their problem-solving skills and achieve more effective and sustainable solutions.

Let's Apply Problem Solving Skills to Real-World Examples

The Workplace Conflict: In an office, there is frequent conflict among team members. The conflict is a symptom, but through careful examination, it is revealed that a lack of clear communication and unclear role definitions are the root causes.

1. Define the Problem:

• Clear Communication and Role Definitions: Clearly identify the lack of clear communication and unclear role definitions as the root causes of the frequent conflicts among team members.

• SMART Goals: Establish specific, measurable, achievable, relevant, and time-bound goals for improving communication and role clarity.

2. Generate Potential Solutions:

• Brainstorming: Encourage team members to share ideas on improving communication and clarifying roles.

• Eliminate Infeasible Solutions: Remove options that do not address the identified root causes.

• List Preferred Solutions: Prioritize solutions that enhance communication and role clarity.

3. Evaluate Alternatives:

• Decision Making: Assess the challenges and benefits of the top solutions.

• Consider Multiple Views: Gather input from team members to ensure a comprehensive evaluation.

4. Decide on a Solution:

• Choose Solutions: Select solutions that focus on improving communication and role definitions.

• Specify Actions: Define steps for enhancing communication and clarifying roles.

• Assign Responsibilities: Identify team members responsible for implementing the chosen solutions.

5. Implement Solution:

• Plan Execution: Develop a detailed plan for implementing changes to communication and role definitions.

• Implementation: Execute the plan, ensuring that team members understand and adopt the improvements.

6. Evaluate the Outcome:

• Assess Effectiveness: Evaluate whether the changes have reduced conflicts and improved team dynamics.

• Consider Revisions: If necessary, revise the plan based on feedback and evolving circumstances.

7. Review What Happened:

• Identify Barriers: Explore any obstacles that hindered the effective implementation of solutions.

• Examine Attitude/Emotion: Consider the impact of attitudes or emotions on the success of the interventions.

• Reflect on Problem-Solving Style: Evaluate the effectiveness of the chosen problem-solving approach.

• Consider Other Problems: Acknowledge any additional issues that may surface during the resolution process.

This real-world example demonstrates how the seven key steps can be applied to address workplace conflict by identifying and resolving underlying issues related to communication and role clarity. The systematic approach ensures a comprehensive and sustainable solution to the recurring problem.

Health and Lifestyle: Suppose someone is experiencing chronic fatigue. The fatigue is the symptom, but after consulting with a healthcare professional and conducting tests, it is determined that poor sleep patterns and an imbalanced diet are the root causes.

1. Define the Problem:

• Chronic Fatigue, Poor Sleep Patterns, and Imbalanced Diet: Clearly identify chronic fatigue as the symptom and poor sleep patterns along with an imbalanced diet as the root causes.

• SMART Goals: Establish specific, measurable, achievable, relevant, and time-bound goals for improving sleep patterns and dietary habits.

2. Generate Potential Solutions:

• Brainstorming: Explore various strategies to address poor sleep patterns and imbalanced diet.

• Eliminate Infeasible Solutions: Rule out options that do not directly address the identified root causes.

• List Preferred Solutions: Prioritize solutions that focus on improving sleep and dietary habits.

3. Evaluate Alternatives:

• Decision Making: Assess the challenges and benefits of the top solutions.

- Consider Multiple Views: Seek input from healthcare professionals and possibly a nutritionist to ensure a comprehensive evaluation.

4. Decide on a Solution:

- Choose Solutions: Select solutions that target improving sleep patterns and establishing a balanced diet.

- Specify Actions: Define specific steps for implementing changes in sleep and dietary habits.

- Assign Responsibilities: If necessary, involve healthcare professionals or a nutritionist in guiding the individual through the changes.

5. Implement Solution:

- Plan Execution: Develop a detailed plan for incorporating the changes into daily life.

- Implementation: Act on the plan, making adjustments to sleep routines and dietary choices.

6. Evaluate the Outcome:

• Assess Effectiveness: Monitor the impact of changes on overall energy levels and fatigue.

• Consider Revisions: If needed, adjust the plan based on feedback and ongoing assessment.

7. Review What Happened:

• Identify Barriers: Explore any obstacles or challenges faced during the implementation of lifestyle changes.

• Examine Attitude/Emotion: Consider the impact of attitudes or emotions on the success of the lifestyle modifications.

• Reflect on Problem-Solving Style: Evaluate the effectiveness of the chosen problem-solving approach.

• Consider Other Problems: Acknowledge any additional health factors that may influence overall well-being and energy levels.

This real-world example illustrates how the seven key steps can be applied to address chronic fatigue by identifying and addressing the underlying issues related to sleep patterns and dietary habits. The systematic approach ensures a comprehensive and sustainable solution to the health concern.

Practical Problem Identification Exercises

Problem Tree Analysis: Create a visual representation of a problem tree. Begin with the problem at the top, and identify branches representing symptoms and roots representing causes. This exercise helps clarify the relationship between symptoms and root causes.

Let's create a hypothetical Problem Tree Analysis for the issue of "Anxiety and Depression."

Problem: Anxiety and Depression

Symptoms (Branches):

- Persistent feelings of sadness

- Difficulty concentrating

- Changes in appetite and sleep patterns

- Social withdrawal and isolation

Root Causes (Roots):

- Biological Factors:

- Genetic predisposition to mental health disorders

- Neurochemical imbalances in the brain

- Psychological Factors:

- Past traumatic experiences

- Chronic stress and unresolved conflicts

- Environmental Factors:

- Lack of social support

- High-pressure work or academic environment

- Lifestyle Factors:

- Unhealthy coping mechanisms

- Substance abuse

- Cultural and Societal Factors:

- Stigma around mental health

- Societal expectations and pressures

Visualization of the Problem Tree:

Anxiety and Depression

```
              /        \

            /          \

          /            \
```

Biological Factors   Psychological Factors

```
      /      \              /      \

    /          \          /          \
```

Genetic Predisposition   Neurochemical Imbalances   Past
Traumatic Experiences

Environmental Factors

/   \

/   \

Lack of Social Support   High-pressure Work or
Academic Environment

Lifestyle Factors

/   \

/   \

Unhealthy Coping Mechanisms   Substance Abuse

Cultural and Societal Factors

```
        /                        \

       /                          \


    Stigma around Mental Health       Societal Expectations and
Pressures
```

This Problem Tree Analysis visually represents the relationship between symptoms and root causes of anxiety and depression. It highlights various factors, including biological, psychological, environmental, lifestyle, and cultural aspects, contributing to the manifestation of anxiety and depression symptoms. This structured overview can aid in identifying areas for intervention, support, and prevention strategies.

Scenario Analysis for Workplace Burnout:

Problem: High levels of workplace burnout among team members.

Scenario 1: Excessive Workload

- Analysis:

- Symptom or Root Cause: Root Cause

- Explanation: An excessive workload can lead to burnout by overwhelming individuals and preventing them from managing their responsibilities effectively. It's a root cause that directly contributes to burnout.

Scenario 2: Lack of Recognition and Appreciation

- Analysis:

- Symptom or Root Cause: Symptom

- Explanation: The lack of recognition and appreciation is a symptom of a deeper issue. While it may contribute to burnout, it is not the root cause. The root cause may involve systemic issues related to leadership and organizational culture.

Scenario 3: Poor Work-Life Balance

- Analysis:

- Symptom or Root Cause: Root Cause

- Explanation: Poor work-life balance is a root cause contributing to burnout. When individuals struggle to maintain a healthy balance between work and personal life, it can lead to chronic stress and burnout.

Scenario 4: Ineffective Communication Channels

- Analysis:

- Symptom or Root Cause: Symptom

- Explanation: Ineffective communication is a symptom that may exacerbate burnout. While it can contribute to workplace stress, the root cause may involve broader issues, such as organizational communication structures and leadership practices.

Scenario 5: Limited Professional Development Opportunities

- Analysis:

- Symptom or Root Cause: Symptom

- Explanation: Limited professional development opportunities can be a symptom of an organizational issue. While it may contribute to burnout, the root cause could involve broader aspects of organizational culture and support for employee growth.

Peer Review:

Seeking input from colleagues, friends, or mentors can provide valuable perspectives on the workplace burnout issue:

Colleague Perspective:

• Insights: Colleagues may highlight specific aspects of the work environment, team dynamics, or leadership that contribute to burnout.

• Feedback: Their input can help identify additional scenarios or nuances in the problem analysis.

Friend Perspective:

• Insights: Friends outside the workplace may offer an objective viewpoint, considering factors that colleagues might overlook.

• Feedback: They may provide insights into the impact of burnout on overall well-being and offer suggestions for improvement.

Mentor Perspective:

• Insights: Mentors with experience in leadership or organizational development can provide strategic insights into addressing burnout.

- Feedback: Their guidance can include actionable steps and long-term solutions to alleviate burnout and create a healthier work environment.

Combining scenario analysis with peer review enhances the depth of understanding of workplace burnout, ensuring a more comprehensive and collaborative approach to problem identification and resolution.

By honing your problem-identification skills, you will set the stage for more effective and targeted problem-solving. You'll be better equipped to tackle challenges at their source, leading to more sustainable solutions and a deeper understanding of the complexities that underlie the problems you encounter. In the chapters that follow, we will continue to refine our problem-solving process, moving from identification to analysis and solution generation.

Step 4: Analyzing Challenges with Precision

Problem analysis is at the heart of effective problem-solving. In this step, we will delve into various analytical techniques that enable us to dissect problems methodically. We'll uncover the power of critical thinking, root cause analysis, and systems thinking. By developing our analytical prowess, we'll gain insight into the intricacies of complex challenges.

The Significance of Problem Analysis

Imagine a detective investigating a complex case. To solve it, the detective must meticulously gather evidence, scrutinize details, and piece together a comprehensive understanding of the situation. Similarly, problem analysis is the process of unraveling the layers of complexity in the challenges we face. It involves examining problems from multiple angles and seeking to understand their causes and implications thoroughly.

Analytical Techniques for Problem-Solving

Critical Thinking: Critical thinking involves evaluating information objectively and making reasoned judgments. It prompts us to question assumptions, consider alternative viewpoints, and assess the credibility of information. Developing critical thinking skills enhances our ability to analyze problems effectively.

Root Cause Analysis: Root cause analysis seeks to identify the fundamental reasons behind a problem. It involves asking "Why?" repeatedly to trace a problem back to its origin. By addressing root causes, we can prevent problems from recurring.

Systems Thinking: Systems thinking views problems as part of a larger system. It considers how various elements within a system interact with and influence each other. This holistic approach helps us understand the broader context in which problems arise.

Real-World Problem Analysis

Environmental Pollution: Consider the problem of environmental pollution. Critical thinking may involve analyzing the impact of different industries, root cause analysis may identify lax regulations as a root cause, and systems thinking may reveal the interconnectedness of pollution with other environmental issues.

Customer Complaints in Business: In a business context, customer complaints are a common issue. Critical thinking may involve examining customer feedback, root cause analysis may uncover product quality issues, and systems thinking may reveal how various departments contribute to or mitigate customer complaints.

Practical Exercises for Problem Analysis

Fishbone Diagram: Create a fishbone diagram (also known as an Ishikawa or cause-and-effect diagram) to identify potential causes of a problem. This visual tool helps you explore different factors contributing to the issue.

Let's create a hypothetical Fishbone Diagram to identify potential causes of the problem "Low Employee Morale and Well-being" in a workplace, focusing on problem-solving, growth, and enhancing mental health.

Problem: Low Employee Morale and Well-being

Fishbone Diagram:

Low Employee Morale and Well-being

```
        /           \

       /             \
```

Work-Related Factors   Personal and Lifestyle Factors

```
    /      \           /        \

   /        \         /          \
```

Lack of Growth   Ineffective   Lack of Work-Life   Personal Stress

Opportunities   Problem-Solving   Balance

Low Employee Morale and Well-being

```
              |

      ---------------------

      |              |
```

Organizational   Individual Factors

Analysis:

Work-Related Factors:

- Lack of Growth Opportunities:

- Root Cause

- Explanation: A lack of opportunities for professional and personal growth can contribute to dissatisfaction and low morale among employees.

- Ineffective Problem-Solving:

- Root Cause

- Explanation: Inability to address and solve workplace challenges effectively can lead to frustration and impact employee well-being.

Personal and Lifestyle Factors:

- Lack of Work-Life Balance:

- Root Cause

- Explanation: A lack of balance between work and personal life can result in increased stress and reduced overall well-being.

- Personal Stress:

- Symptom

- Explanation: While personal stress is a symptom, the root cause could be a combination of work-related and personal factors.

Organizational Factors:

- Culture of Continuous Learning:

- Root Cause

- Explanation: A lack of emphasis on a culture of continuous learning and development can impact employee engagement and morale.

- Communication Gaps:

- Root Cause

- Explanation: Ineffective communication channels within the organization can lead to misunderstandings, contributing to lower morale.

Individual Factors:

- Resilience and Coping Skills:

- External Factor

- Explanation: Individual differences in resilience and coping skills may impact how employees respond to stressors and challenges.

The Fishbone Diagram visually represents potential causes of low employee morale and well-being, categorizing them into work-related factors, personal and lifestyle factors, organizational factors, and individual factors. This tool helps in systematically exploring different dimensions of the problem, facilitating a more comprehensive understanding of the contributing factors and guiding interventions for improvement.

SWOT Analysis for Employee Burnout:

Internal Factors:

Strengths:

• Dedicated Workforce: Employees are committed and dedicated to their work.

• Team Collaboration: Strong collaboration and teamwork within departments.

• Existing Employee Support Programs: Presence of existing support programs for employee well-being.

Weaknesses:

• Lack of Work-Life Balance: Many employees struggle with maintaining a healthy work-life balance.

• Communication Challenges: Inadequate communication channels leading to misunderstandings.

• Limited Professional Development: Opportunities for growth and development are limited.

External Factors:

Opportunities:

- Flexible Work Arrangements: Opportunities to introduce flexible work arrangements.

- Wellness Programs: Implementing comprehensive wellness programs to support mental health.

- External Training Resources: Leveraging external resources for professional development.

Threats:

- Industry Competition: High competition in the industry, leading to increased workload and stress.

- Economic Downturn: Economic uncertainties impacting job security and morale.

- Limited Access to Mental Health Resources: Lack of external resources for mental health support.

Scenario Planning for Employee Burnout:

Scenario 1: Best-Case Scenario

- Effective Implementation of Wellness Programs:

- Increased employee engagement and well-being.

- Improved work-life balance.

- Enhanced job satisfaction and productivity.

Scenario 2: Moderate Scenario

- Introduction of Flexible Work Arrangements:

- Moderate improvement in work-life balance.

- Some resistance or challenges in adapting to new work arrangements.

- Incremental improvement in employee morale.

Scenario 3: Worst-Case Scenario

- Economic Downturn Leading to Layoffs:

- Increased stress and anxiety among employees due to job insecurity.

- Decline in morale and team collaboration.

- Potential negative impact on the company's overall culture.

Key Takeaways:

- The SWOT analysis highlights internal strengths and weaknesses, as well as external opportunities and threats, providing a comprehensive understanding of factors influencing employee burnout.

- Scenario planning allows for a nuanced exploration of potential outcomes, from positive to challenging situations, guiding the development of proactive strategies to address and prevent burnout.

Combining SWOT analysis with scenario planning creates a robust framework for understanding and addressing employee burnout, ensuring a strategic and comprehensive approach to problem-solving and well-being improvement.

By honing your problem analysis skills, you will become better equipped to deconstruct complex challenges and identify effective solutions. Problem analysis is the bridge between problem identification and solution generation, and it serves as a critical step in the problem-solving process. In the chapters that follow, we will continue to refine our problem-solving toolkit, moving from analysis to solution generation and implementation.

Section 3: The Creative Spark: Generating Solutions

Step 5: Igniting Creativity in Problem Solving

Creativity is the spark that ignites innovative solutions. In this step, we will tap into our creative potential and explore techniques to foster creative problem-solving. From brainstorming to lateral thinking, we'll uncover the myriad ways creativity can lead us to novel solutions. Through practical exercises, we will awaken our creative faculties.

The Role of Creativity in Problem-Solving

Creativity is the force that propels us beyond conventional solutions, opening the door to fresh ideas and breakthrough innovations. When we embrace creativity in problem-solving, we liberate ourselves from the constraints of tradition and explore uncharted territories of possibility.

Techniques for Fostering Creativity

Brainstorming: Brainstorming is a classic technique that encourages the generation of a wide range of ideas without judgment. It thrives on free association and encourages participants to think creatively without limitations.

Lateral Thinking: Lateral thinking, a term coined by Edward de Bono, involves approaching problems from unconventional angles. It encourages thinking "outside the box" and challenges established thought patterns.

Mind Mapping: Mind mapping is a visual technique that helps organize thoughts and ideas around a central concept or problem. It fosters creativity by allowing us to make connections and explore associations between different elements.

Role Reversal: Role reversal is a technique where individuals step into the shoes of someone with a different perspective or role. This exercise helps generate fresh insights by viewing the problem from a new vantage point.

Practical Exercises to Ignite Creativity

Random Word Association: Select a random word and associate it with your problem. Use this word as a springboard to generate creative ideas and solutions.

Six Thinking Hats: Inspired by Edward de Bono, the Six Thinking Hats technique assigns different "hats" or roles to participants, encouraging them to approach the problem from various angles such as creativity, emotion, and logic.

Metaphorical Thinking: Compare your problem to something completely unrelated. How might your problem be similar to, for example, a journey, a piece of music, or a natural phenomenon? This exercise can reveal novel perspectives.

Collaborative Creativity: Organize brainstorming sessions or creative workshops with colleagues or friends. Collaborative creativity often results in a synergy of ideas and sparks innovative solutions.

Embracing the Creative Process

It's important to recognize that creativity is not a switch that can be turned on and off at will. It's a process that thrives on curiosity, experimentation, and a willingness to embrace failure as part of the journey.

As we awaken our creative faculties in problem-solving, we will discover that creativity is not a finite resource; it is a boundless wellspring within each of us. By infusing creativity into our problem-solving process, we empower ourselves to approach challenges with fresh perspectives and inventive solutions. In the chapters that follow, we will continue to explore how creativity, combined with analytical skills, can lead us to effective problem resolution and personal growth.

Step 6: The Toolbox of Solutions

Every problem-solving journey requires a well-equipped toolbox filled with a diverse range of problem-solving techniques. In this step, we will populate our toolbox with an array of problem-solving methods. We'll explore structured techniques such as the 5 Whys, SWOT analysis, decision matrices, and more. By expanding our repertoire of problem-solving tools, we become versatile and effective problem solvers.

The Value of a Diverse Toolbox

Imagine a skilled craftsman with a toolbox containing a wide variety of tools. Each tool serves a unique purpose, allowing the craftsman to tackle different aspects of a project with precision and efficiency. Similarly, in problem-solving, having a diverse toolbox of techniques equips us to address a broad spectrum of challenges.

Structured Problem-Solving Methods

The 5 Whys: The 5 Whys technique involves repeatedly asking "Why?" to uncover the root cause of a problem. By iteratively probing deeper into the issue, we can identify the underlying causes and address them directly.

The 5 Whys:

Sample Problem: High defect rates in a manufacturing process.

Why are there high defect rates?

- Because the quality control checks are not catching issues during production.

Why are the quality control checks ineffective?

- Because the inspection process is not thorough enough.

Why is the inspection process not thorough?

- Because the inspection team lacks specific training on identifying certain types of defects.

Why is there a lack of training for the inspection team?

- Because there is no formal training program in place.

Why is there no formal training program for the inspection team?

- Because the company has not recognized the need for structured training in quality control.

In this example, the 5 Whys lead to the root cause, which is the absence of a formal training program in quality control. Addressing this root cause can potentially reduce the defect rates.

SWOT Analysis: SWOT (Strengths, Weaknesses, Opportunities, Threats) analysis is a framework for assessing the internal and external factors influencing a situation. It helps us identify potential solutions by leveraging strengths, addressing weaknesses, seizing opportunities, and mitigating threats.

SWOT Analysis:

Sample Scenario: Analyzing the situation of a small business entering a new market.

- Strengths:

- Established brand reputation.

- Strong financial position.

- Weaknesses:

- Limited experience in the new market.

- Lack of established distribution channels.

- Opportunities:

- Growing demand for the product in the new market.

- Untapped customer segments.

- Threats:

- Intense competition from local businesses.

- Economic uncertainties in the new market.

The SWOT analysis helps in formulating a strategy by leveraging strengths, addressing weaknesses, seizing opportunities, and mitigating threats for a successful market entry.

Decision Matrices: Decision matrices provide a structured approach to evaluating and comparing different options. By assigning weights to criteria and scoring each option, we can make informed decisions based on a systematic analysis.

Decision Matrices:

Sample Decision: Choosing a project management software for a team.

Criteria:

- User-friendliness (Weight: 30%)

- Feature set (Weight: 40%)

- Cost (Weight: 20%)

- Customer support (Weight: 10%)

Options:

- Software A

- Software B

- Software C

Scoring:

- Software A: 8, 9, $150/month, 7

- Software B: 7, 8, $200/month, 8

- Software C: 9, 7, $180/month, 9

Weighted Scores:

- Software A: $(8 * 0.3) + (9 * 0.4) + (150 * 0.2) + (7 * 0.1) = 7.9$

- Software B: $(7 * 0.3) + (8 * 0.4) + (200 * 0.2) + (8 * 0.1) = 7.8$

- Software C: $(9 * 0.3) + (7 * 0.4) + (180 * 0.2) + (9 * 0.1) = 8.1$

Based on the weighted scores, Software C emerges as the preferred option for the team.

These structured problem-solving methods provide systematic approaches to understanding, analyzing, and resolving issues in various contexts.

Creative Problem-Solving Techniques

Mind mapping: is a visual technique that serves as a powerful tool for organizing thoughts and ideas in a non-linear and creative manner. The process revolves around a central concept or problem, with branches radiating outward to represent related concepts, associations, or solutions. This method is instrumental in facilitating a visual representation of information, enabling individuals to see connections, identify patterns, and stimulate creative thinking.

Key Components of Mind Mapping:

Central Theme:

- The core concept or problem is placed at the center of the mind map, serving as the focal point for exploration.

Branches:

- Radiating from the central theme, branches represent different categories, ideas, or aspects related to the main concept.

Nodes:

- Nodes on each branch contain specific details, thoughts, or subtopics associated with the overarching theme.

Colors and Images:

- Incorporating colors and images enhances visual memory and stimulates creative thinking.

Advantages of Mind Mapping:

Visualization:

- Offers a visual representation of complex information, making it easier to comprehend and remember.

Creativity:

- Facilitates the generation of creative ideas by encouraging a non-linear approach to problem-solving.

Organization:

- Provides a structured and organized framework for thoughts and ideas, promoting clarity.

Connection Recognition:

- Helps identify relationships and connections between different concepts, fostering a holistic understanding.

Brainstorming:

- Ideal for brainstorming sessions, allowing for the free-flowing exploration of ideas.

Example:

Central Theme: Sustainable Living

- Branches:

- Energy Conservation

- Waste Reduction

- Eco-friendly Transportation

- Green Building Practices

- Nodes:

- Energy-Efficient Appliances

- Recycling Programs

- Bicycle Commuting

- Use of Renewable Materials in Construction

By employing mind mapping, individuals can visually explore the various facets of sustainable living, uncover connections between different elements, and generate innovative solutions to promote eco-friendly practices.

TRIZ, the Theory of Inventive Problem Solving, stands as a systematic methodology for innovation and problem-solving. This approach offers a comprehensive set of principles and inventive patterns meticulously designed to address and overcome various technical challenges. By harnessing TRIZ, individuals and teams gain a structured framework to navigate complexities, fostering a more efficient and creative problem-solving process in the realm of innovation and technology.

Let's consider a simplified example applying TRIZ principles:

Problem: Enhance the efficiency of a manual door-closing mechanism.

TRIZ Principles Applied:

Principle of Segmentation: Divide the door into smaller segments, allowing for more controlled and precise closing.

Principle of Local Quality: Focus on improving the closing mechanism in a specific area, enhancing the overall performance.

Principle of Asymmetry: Introduce an asymmetrical design that facilitates a smoother closing motion.

Principle of Dynamics: Implement a dynamic closing mechanism that adapts to different door weights and sizes.

Principle of Intermediary: Include an intermediary component that optimizes the force applied during the closing process.

Principle of Inversion: Explore unconventional approaches, such as having the door close from the bottom-up rather than top-down.

Principle of Feedback: Integrate a feedback system that adjusts the closing force based on real-time conditions.

By applying these TRIZ principles, one can systematically explore innovative solutions to enhance the manual door-closing mechanism, ultimately improving efficiency and addressing the initial problem.

Design Thinking: is a human-centered problem-solving approach that prioritizes the needs and experiences of users. At its core, this methodology revolves around empathy, ideation, and prototyping to cultivate innovative solutions. By immersing itself in the user's perspective, Design Thinking ensures that the resulting solutions are not only functional but also resonate with the intended audience. The iterative process of brainstorming and prototyping encourages a dynamic and flexible approach, allowing for the refinement and optimization of ideas until a well-suited and user-centric solution emerges. In essence, Design Thinking is a collaborative and creative framework that seeks to understand, ideate, and implement solutions that genuinely address the challenges faced by the end-users.

Let's consider a practical example applying Design Thinking:

Problem Statement: Improve the experience of public transportation for commuters in a busy urban setting.

Design Thinking Process:

Empathize:

• Conduct interviews, surveys, and observations to understand the daily challenges and frustrations of commuters.

• Identify pain points such as overcrowded buses, confusing schedules, and uncomfortable waiting areas.

Define:

- Clearly articulate the specific problems faced by commuters, such as long wait times, lack of real-time information, and discomfort during the journey.

Ideate:

- Brainstorm creative solutions collaboratively with a diverse team.

- Generate ideas like a mobile app for real-time bus tracking, modular and comfortable bus interiors, and community engagement initiatives to enhance the waiting experience.

Prototype:

- Develop a low-fidelity prototype of the mobile app to visualize the real-time tracking feature.

- Create a model or simulation of a redesigned bus interior that maximizes comfort and usability.

Test:

- Gather feedback from a sample group of commuters using the prototype app.

- Seek input on the proposed bus interior design through surveys or interactive sessions.

Iterate:

- Refine the solutions based on user feedback.

- Modify the app interface for better usability and incorporate suggested improvements for the bus interior.

Implement:

- Roll out the improved public transportation experience, integrating the mobile app and redesigned bus interiors.

- Monitor and collect ongoing feedback for continuous refinement.

By employing the principles of Design Thinking, the process focuses not only on solving the surface-level issues but also on creating a holistic and user-centered solution that enhances the overall commuting experience.

Practical Application and Versatility

To enhance our problem-solving toolbox you must:

Learn: Invest time in understanding and mastering each technique. Explore books, courses, or online resources that delve into the specific methods.

Practice: Apply these techniques to real-world problems. The more you practice, the more proficient you become in choosing the right tool for each challenge.

Combine: Don't limit yourself to a single technique. Often, a combination of methods can yield the most effective solutions. Experiment with different approaches as you tackle complex problems.

Seek Feedback: Collaborate with others to gain diverse perspectives on which tools are most suitable for a given problem. Feedback and discussions can enrich your problem-solving process.

Becoming a Versatile Problem Solver

As you expand your problem-solving toolbox, you become a versatile problem solver capable of adapting to a wide range of challenges. The ability to select the right tool for the job and apply it effectively is a hallmark of effective problem solvers. In the chapters that follow, we will continue to refine our problem-solving skills, moving from tool selection to solution implementation and, ultimately, to personal growth and resilience.

Section 4: Implementing Solutions with Precision

Step 7: Planning and Execution

A well-crafted solution is only effective if it's put into action. In this step, we'll delve into the crucial planning and execution phase of problem-solving. We'll learn to create action plans, set milestones, and track progress. By mastering this aspect of problem-solving, we ensure that our solutions translate into real-world results.

The Critical Role of Planning and Execution

Imagine an architect who has designed a magnificent building. However, without skilled construction workers to bring the design to life and meticulous planning to guide the process, the building remains a blueprint. Similarly, in problem-solving, our solutions are like blueprints. Planning and execution are the construction phase—the bridge between ideas and tangible results.

Creating Effective Action Plans

Clear Objectives: Define the specific objectives your solution aims to achieve. What is the desired outcome? Having clear objectives ensures everyone understands the goal.

Detailed Tasks: Break down the solution into actionable tasks or steps. These should be specific, measurable, and time-bound.

Assigned Responsibilities: Identify who will be responsible for each task. Clear accountability ensures that everyone knows their role in the execution.

Timelines and Milestones: Set timelines for each task and establish milestones to track progress. This helps prevent delays and ensures steady progress toward the goal.

Resource Allocation: Determine the resources required for each task, including personnel, budget, equipment, and materials.

Tracking Progress and Adaptation

Regular Check-Ins: Schedule regular check-in meetings to review progress, discuss challenges, and make necessary adjustments. Communication is key to successful execution.

Problem-Solving During Execution: Be prepared to adapt your plan as unexpected challenges arise. Problem-solving during execution ensures that you can overcome obstacles on the path to your goal.

Feedback Loops: Establish feedback mechanisms to collect input from team members and stakeholders. Feedback helps identify areas for improvement and refinement.

Monitoring and Evaluation

Key Performance Indicators (KPIs): Define KPIs that will be used to measure the success of your solution. KPIs should align with your objectives and be quantifiable.

Data Collection: Collect relevant data and metrics to assess progress and outcomes. Ensure data is accurate, timely, and reliable.

Continuous Improvement: Use the data and feedback collected to continuously improve your solution and the execution process. Adaptation and refinement are essential for success.

Communication and Transparency

Stakeholder Engagement: Keep stakeholders informed about progress and developments. Transparency builds trust and fosters collaboration.

Effective Communication: Ensure that communication within the team is clear and that everyone is aligned with the execution plan.

Celebrate Milestones: Recognize and celebrate achievements and milestones along the way. This boosts morale and motivation.

Adapting to Change

In today's dynamic world, adaptability is crucial. Be prepared to adjust your action plan and solutions as circumstances change. Flexibility and the ability to pivot when necessary are hallmarks of effective execution.

Conclusion: Transforming Ideas into Reality

As we master the planning and execution phase of problem-solving, we transform ideas into reality. Solutions take shape, objectives are achieved, and progress is made. This step is the culmination of our problem-solving journey, where our efforts translate into meaningful results.

In the chapters that follow, we will explore the impact of effective problem-solving not only on the challenges we face but also on our personal growth and resilience. By mastering the entire problem-solving process, from identification to execution, we become empowered problem solvers capable of making a tangible difference in our lives and the world around us.

Step 8: Learning from Every Solution

Every problem we solve offers valuable lessons. In this step, we will embrace the idea that problems are opportunities for growth. We'll explore how to conduct post-mortems and retrospectives, extracting insights from our problem-solving experiences. By adopting a continuous learning approach, we become more adept problem solvers with each challenge we face.

The Growth Mindset in Problem-Solving

In our journey of problem-solving, it's crucial to adopt a growth mindset—a belief that every challenge is an opportunity for learning and improvement. Instead of viewing problems as setbacks, we should see them as stepping stones on our path to personal growth and resilience.

The Importance of Reflection

Reflection is a powerful tool for learning and growth. It allows us to review our experiences, assess outcomes, and identify areas for improvement. In problem-solving, reflection takes the form of post-mortems and retrospectives.

Post-Mortems and Retrospectives

Post-Mortems: Post-mortems are typically conducted at the end of a project or after a significant problem has been resolved. They involve a comprehensive review of what went well and what didn't. The goal is to understand the root causes of issues, acknowledge successes, and make recommendations for future improvements.

Retrospectives: Retrospectives are often used in agile project management methodologies. They are conducted at regular intervals during a project to assess progress, identify obstacles, and plan for adjustments. Retrospectives focus on continuous improvement and adaptability.

Extracting Insights

During post-mortems and retrospectives:

Ask Questions: Encourage open and honest discussion among team members. Ask questions like, "What worked well?", "What didn't go as planned?", and "What can we do differently next time?"

Identify Root Causes: Dig deep to uncover the root causes of any challenges or failures. Avoid blaming individuals and focus on systemic issues.

Acknowledge Successes: Celebrate successes and achievements, no matter how small. Positive reinforcement boosts morale and motivation.

Recommendations for Improvement: Based on the insights gained, make concrete recommendations for improvement. Develop action items that can be implemented in future problem-solving endeavors.

Continuous Learning and Adaptation

The key to growth through problem-solving lies in continuous learning and adaptation. Each problem we encounter is an opportunity to refine our skills, enhance our knowledge, and become more resilient.

Embracing the Journey

As we conclude our problem-solving journey, remember that it is not a linear path with a fixed destination. It is an ongoing journey of self-discovery and personal development. By approaching problems with a growth mindset, conducting post-mortems and retrospectives, and continuously learning from every solution, we become not only more effective problem solvers but also individuals who are better equipped to navigate life's challenges with resilience and wisdom.

In the chapters that follow, we will explore the profound connection between problem-solving, personal growth, and mental well-being. May this journey inspire you to view every problem as an opportunity and every solution as a stepping stone towards a more resilient and empowered self.

As we conclude Chapter 2, we will have journeyed deeper into the problem-solving mindset, honing our ability to approach problems with positivity, adaptability, and creativity. We'll also have a toolbox filled with problem-solving techniques and the knowledge to execute solutions effectively. Armed with these insights and skills, we are ready to tackle the labyrinth of life's challenges with confidence, resilience, and a steadfast commitment to our personal growth and mental well-being.

"The only thing that stands between you and your dream is the will to try and the belief that it is actually possible."

— Joel Brown

Chapter 3: Resilience, Stress, and Problem-Solving

Section 1: The Stress-Resilience Connection

In this chapter, we will explore the intricate relationship between stress, resilience, and problem-solving. We'll delve into how effective problem-solving serves as a buffer against stress and a catalyst for building resilience.

Step 1: The Stress Factor

Stress is an inevitable part of life, but it doesn't have to be a constant burden. In this step, we'll dissect the concept of stress, understanding its different forms and how it impacts our mental and physical well-being. We'll also explore the physiological and psychological responses to stress, laying the foundation for our journey towards stress management through problem-solving.

Understanding Stress

Stress is a natural response to the demands and challenges we encounter in our lives. It can manifest in various forms, from everyday stressors like work deadlines and traffic jams to more significant life events such as relationship issues or major life changes. Stress is a universal experience, and it affects everyone to some degree.

Types of Stress

Acute Stress: This is a short-term form of stress that arises from immediate stressors or challenges. It triggers the body's "fight or flight" response, preparing us to deal with an imminent threat.

Chronic Stress: Chronic stress is long-term and can result from ongoing issues such as financial difficulties, chronic health conditions, or persistent work-related stress. It can take a toll on both physical and mental health.

Episodic Stress: Some individuals frequently experience acute stress due to their lifestyle or personality. These episodic stressors can lead to chronic stress if they are not managed effectively.

The Impact of Stress

Stress can affect us in multiple ways:

Physical Health: Prolonged stress can lead to various physical health issues, including high blood pressure, heart disease, gastrointestinal problems, and a weakened immune system.

Mental Health: Stress is closely linked to mental health conditions such as anxiety disorders, depression, and burnout. It can exacerbate existing mental health challenges and lead to the development of new ones.

Cognitive Function: Chronic stress can impair cognitive function, affecting memory, concentration, and decision-making abilities.

Behavioral Changes: People under stress may exhibit changes in behavior, including increased irritability, changes in sleep patterns, and unhealthy coping mechanisms such as overeating or substance abuse.

Physiological and Psychological Responses to Stress

Understanding the body's and mind's responses to stress is crucial to managing it effectively:

Fight or Flight Response: When faced with a stressor, the body releases stress hormones like cortisol and adrenaline. These hormones prepare the body to respond by increasing heart rate, sharpening focus, and diverting resources to essential functions.

Psychological Responses: Stress can lead to various psychological responses, including heightened anxiety, worry, and feelings of helplessness. It can also manifest as physical symptoms like headaches or muscle tension.

The Role of Problem-Solving in Stress Management

Problem-solving is a powerful tool in managing stress. By addressing the root causes of stressors and developing effective coping strategies, we can reduce the impact of stress on our mental and physical well-being. In the chapters that follow, we will explore how problem-solving can be applied to various aspects of life to enhance stress management and promote mental health and resilience.

Step 2: The Resilience Perspective

Resilience isn't just about bouncing back from stress; it's about thriving in its presence. In this step, we'll examine resilience from a fresh perspective. We'll learn how individuals with high resilience not only weather the storm but also grow through adversity. Through real-life stories and psychological insights, we'll grasp the essence of resilience as a dynamic, learnable skill.

Understanding Resilience

Resilience is often likened to the ability to "bounce back" from life's challenges, and while that's certainly a part of it, it's not the whole story. Resilience is a multi-faceted skill that allows individuals not only to withstand adversity but also to learn, adapt, and even flourish in its presence.

The Resilience Spectrum

Resilience exists on a spectrum, ranging from low resilience, where individuals struggle to cope with even minor stressors, to high resilience, where individuals thrive amidst significant adversity. It's a skill that can be developed and strengthened over time.

Growing Through Adversity

Highly resilient individuals often experience growth through adversity. This phenomenon is known as "post-traumatic growth" or "adversarial growth." It means that, in the face of challenges, people can emerge even stronger, wiser, and more compassionate than before.

Psychological Insights

Resilience is deeply intertwined with our psychological responses to stress and adversity:

Cognitive Flexibility: Resilient individuals tend to be more mentally flexible. They can reframe challenges, finding opportunities for learning and growth even in difficult situations.

Emotional Regulation: Resilience involves the ability to regulate emotions effectively. Instead of being overwhelmed by negative emotions, resilient individuals can manage them constructively.

Positive Mindset: Maintaining a positive outlook, even in the face of adversity, is a hallmark of resilience. It's the belief that, even in challenging times, better days lie ahead.

Real-Life Stories of Resilience

The Entrepreneur's Comeback: After a failed startup, John faced financial ruin and the emotional toll of his business's collapse. Instead of giving up, he used the experience as a learning opportunity. He started a new venture, applying the lessons he had learned, and eventually achieved remarkable success.

The Survivor's Strength: Jane survived a life-threatening illness that left her physically and emotionally scarred. Through therapy and a support network, she not only recovered but also became an advocate for others facing similar challenges, channeling her experience into a mission to help others.

The Dynamic Nature of Resilience

Resilience isn't a fixed trait; it's a dynamic skill that can be developed and refined throughout life. By embracing the resilience perspective, we open ourselves up to the possibility of not only surviving adversity but also thriving because of it.

In the chapters that follow, we'll explore how problem-solving can be a powerful tool in developing and enhancing resilience. We'll discover how the skills we've cultivated can be applied to build a strong foundation for mental well-being and personal growth.

Section 2: Problem-Solving as a Stress Reduction Tool

Step 3: Stress Reduction through Problem-Solving

Effective problem-solving isn't just about finding solutions; it's also a potent stress-reduction tool. In this step, we'll delve into how approaching problems with a structured mindset can alleviate stress. We'll learn to transform stressors into solvable challenges and develop a sense of control over our circumstances. We'll explore practical strategies for using problem-solving to reduce stress in our daily lives.

The Connection Between Problem-Solving and Stress

Stress often arises from the perception of a problem without a clear solution. This feeling of helplessness or uncertainty can be a significant source of stress. Effective problem-solving offers a structured approach to addressing these challenges, thereby reducing stress.

Transforming Stressors into Challenges

Identify the Stressor: The first step is to identify the specific stressor causing distress. Is it a work-related problem, a personal issue, or an external circumstance like traffic?

Reframe as a Challenge: Instead of viewing the situation as an insurmountable stressor, reframe it as a solvable challenge. Challenges are opportunities for growth and problem-solving.

Break It Down: Divide the challenge into smaller, manageable components. This step-by-step approach makes the challenge less overwhelming.

Developing a Sense of Control

A significant source of stress is the feeling of being out of control. Problem-solving empowers individuals by giving them a sense of control over their circumstances.

Set Clear Goals: Clearly define what you want to achieve through problem-solving. Having a specific goal in mind helps focus your efforts.

Identify Possible Solutions: Brainstorm potential solutions to the challenge. Consider different approaches and alternatives.

Create an Action Plan: Develop a step-by-step action plan to implement the chosen solution. This plan provides a clear roadmap for addressing the challenge.

Take Action: Act on your plan. Taking even small steps towards a solution can alleviate stress by demonstrating progress.

Practical Strategies for Stress Reduction Through Problem-Solving

Time Management: Feeling overwhelmed by a lack of time is a common stressor. Use problem-solving to create a time management plan, prioritizing tasks and allocating time effectively.

Interpersonal Conflicts: Address conflicts with a problem-solving approach. Focus on communication, understanding, and finding common ground.

Financial Stress: Create a budget and financial plan to address money-related stressors. Seek professional advice if necessary.

Health Challenges: When facing health issues, use problem-solving to research treatment options, make informed decisions, and create a self-care plan.

Mindfulness and Problem-Solving

Mindfulness practices can complement problem-solving in stress reduction. Mindfulness helps individuals stay present, reduce anxiety about the future, and make clearer decisions when problem-solving.

Conclusion: Empowerment and Stress Reduction

By viewing stressors as challenges and applying problem-solving techniques, we can regain a sense of control over our lives. Stress reduction through problem-solving is not about eliminating all stress but about building resilience and coping skills to navigate stressors with confidence. In the chapters that follow, we will continue to explore how problem-solving can be applied to various aspects of life to promote mental well-being and personal growth.

Step 4: Problem-Solving for Emotional Regulation

Emotions often run high during stressful times. In this step, we'll explore how problem-solving skills can enhance emotional regulation. We'll discover the power of a rational, solution-oriented mindset in managing emotional responses to stress. Through exercises in emotional intelligence, we'll learn to navigate the turbulent waters of our feelings with greater ease.

The Link Between Emotions and Stress

Stress is intimately connected to our emotions. When we encounter stressors, our emotional responses can range from anxiety and frustration to anger and sadness. Learning to regulate these emotions is essential for effective stress management.

The Rational Mindset

Identifying Emotional Triggers: The first step in emotional regulation is recognizing what triggers our emotions during stressful situations. Is it a specific type of challenge, a particular person, or a recurrent theme in your life?

Pause and Reflect: When emotions flare up, take a moment to pause and reflect. Ask yourself, "What is the source of this emotion?" Identifying the root cause can help you address it more effectively.

Rational Analysis: Apply problem-solving techniques to the situation. What are the facts of the problem? What potential solutions are available? How can you work towards a resolution?

Emotion Validation: Acknowledge and validate your emotions. It's essential to recognize that your feelings are valid and natural responses to stress. Don't judge yourself for feeling a certain way.

Emotional Intelligence Exercises

Mindfulness Meditation: Mindfulness practices, such as meditation, can help you become more aware of your emotions and create space between the emotion and your response to it.

Journaling: Keep a journal to record your emotions and the situations that trigger them. This can help you identify patterns and gain insight into your emotional responses.

Empathy Building: Practice empathy by imagining how others might feel in a given situation. This can help you understand and manage your own emotions better.

Positive Self-Talk: Challenge negative self-talk with positive and rational affirmations. Replace statements like "I can't handle this" with "I can find a solution."

Emotional Regulation as a Resilience Builder

Emotional regulation is a critical aspect of resilience. When we can manage our emotions effectively, we are better equipped to bounce back from setbacks and stay focused on solutions rather than becoming overwhelmed by the challenges we face.

Conclusion: Embracing Emotional Regulation

Emotional regulation is a valuable skill that complements problem-solving in our journey towards stress management, personal growth, and resilience. By cultivating emotional intelligence and adopting a rational mindset, we can navigate the emotional turbulence of stress with greater ease. In the chapters that follow, we will continue to explore how problem-solving can be applied to various aspects of life to promote mental well-being and personal growth.

Section 3: Building Resilience through Problem-Solving

Step 5: Problem-Solving as Resilience Training

Resilience is like a muscle—it strengthens with exercise. In this step, we'll understand how problem-solving acts as resilience training. We'll explore stories of individuals who have used problem-solving to transform adversity into opportunities for growth. We'll also learn to identify stressors as opportunities to enhance our resilience through problem-solving.

The Resilience Muscle

Much like physical muscles, resilience can be developed and strengthened with practice. Problem-solving serves as an effective training ground for resilience because it equips us to face challenges head-on and develop the skills necessary to bounce back from adversity.

Real-Life Stories of Resilience through Problem-Solving

The Career Setback: Sarah faced a major setback in her career when she was unexpectedly laid off from her job. Instead of succumbing to despair, she approached it as an opportunity. She used problem-solving to reevaluate her career goals, update her skills, and explore new opportunities. In the process, she discovered a new passion and eventually started her own successful business.

Health Crisis: Mark was diagnosed with a chronic illness that required significant lifestyle changes. Instead of giving in to despair, he approached it as a problem to solve. He researched his condition, sought expert advice, and developed a comprehensive self-care plan. Over time, not only did he manage his health effectively, but he also became an advocate for others facing similar challenges.

Identifying Stressors as Resilience Opportunities

Recognize Stressors: When faced with a stressor, whether it's a personal setback, a difficult relationship, or a work-related challenge, recognize it as an opportunity for resilience building.

Apply Problem-Solving Skills: Utilize problem-solving techniques to address the stressor. Break it down into manageable components, identify potential solutions, and create a plan of action.

Embrace Growth: Understand that resilience isn't just about overcoming difficulties; it's about growing through them. Every challenge you face and solve contributes to your resilience muscle.

Resilience as an Ongoing Process

Resilience isn't a one-time achievement; it's a continuous journey. The more you practice problem-solving in the face of adversity, the stronger your resilience becomes.

Conclusion: Resilience through Problem-Solving

Problem-solving serves as a dynamic and effective tool for building resilience. By approaching stressors as opportunities for growth, applying problem-solving skills, and learning from real-life stories of resilience, we can develop our resilience muscle. In the chapters that follow, we will continue to explore how problem-solving can be applied to various aspects of life to promote mental well-being and personal growth.

Step 6: Adaptability and Problem-Solving

Adaptability is a key component of resilience. In this step, we'll delve into how effective problem solvers are inherently adaptable. We'll learn to embrace change as an opportunity for growth and resilience building. Through practical exercises, we'll enhance our adaptability skills, ensuring we thrive in a constantly evolving world.

The Connection Between Adaptability and Resilience

Adaptability is the ability to adjust to new conditions and navigate change effectively. It's closely linked to resilience because, in the face of adversity, those who can adapt are more likely to bounce back and thrive.

Embracing Change as an Opportunity

Mindset Shift: Instead of resisting change or viewing it as a threat, shift your mindset to see change as an opportunity for learning and growth.

Embrace Uncertainty: Understand that change often brings uncertainty, and uncertainty can be an opportunity to build resilience. It's a chance to test your problem-solving skills and develop new strategies.

Learn from Challenges: Reflect on past challenges and how you adapted to them. What worked well, and what could be improved? Use this knowledge to enhance your adaptability.

Practical Exercises to Enhance Adaptability

Try Something New: Challenge yourself to try something outside your comfort zone. It could be a new hobby, a different type of exercise, or a new skill. This helps build adaptability by exposing you to change.

Change Your Routine: Make small changes to your daily routine. This could be as simple as rearranging your workspace or trying a new commute. These minor disruptions help train your brain to adapt to change.

Problem-Solving Simulations: Create scenarios where you have to adapt to unexpected changes. Practice finding solutions and making decisions quickly.

Seek Feedback: Ask for feedback from trusted friends, family, or colleagues. They can provide insights into areas where you may need to be more adaptable.

Adaptability as a Resilience Skill

Resourcefulness: Adaptable individuals are resourceful. They can make the most of the resources available to them, whether in a personal or professional context.

Stress Management: Being adaptable can reduce stress because you're better equipped to handle unexpected challenges.

Open-Mindedness: Adaptability often comes with an open-minded approach to new ideas and perspectives. This openness can lead to more effective problem-solving.

Conclusion: Thriving in a Changing World

Adaptability is a critical component of resilience, and it can be cultivated through problem-solving and a willingness to embrace change. By enhancing our adaptability skills, we ensure that we not only survive but thrive in an ever-evolving world. In the chapters that follow, we will continue to explore how problem-solving can be applied to various aspects of life to promote mental well-being and personal growth.

Section 4: Cultivating Resilience through Problem-Solving

Step 7: Problem-Solving and Goal Achievement

Goals are the milestones of personal growth, and they often intersect with stressors. In this step, we'll explore how problem-solving skills can bridge the gap between goal achievement and resilience building. We'll uncover how tackling obstacles with a structured approach propels us toward our goals and simultaneously strengthens our resilience.

The Interplay Between Goals and Resilience

Goals are powerful motivators in our lives. Whether they are related to career advancement, personal development, or health and well-being, goals provide a sense of purpose and direction. However, the path to achieving these goals is often riddled with challenges and setbacks.

Problem-Solving as a Goal Achievement Tool

Goal Setting: Start by setting clear and achievable goals. Clearly defining what you want to accomplish provides a roadmap for problem-solving.

Identify Potential Obstacles: Anticipate the challenges and obstacles that may arise on your path to achieving the goal. This proactive approach allows you to address issues as they emerge.

Problem-Solving Strategies: Apply problem-solving techniques to overcome obstacles. Break down challenges into smaller components and work through them systematically.

Adaptation: Be willing to adapt your approach if a particular strategy isn't working. Problem-solving includes the flexibility to adjust your tactics as needed.

Real-Life Examples

Career Advancement: John aimed for a promotion at work. When he faced unexpected resistance from colleagues, he used problem-solving to address interpersonal conflicts, build alliances, and demonstrate his capabilities. Ultimately, he achieved his goal and enhanced his resilience by navigating workplace challenges.

Fitness Journey: Sarah wanted to improve her fitness and lose weight. She encountered plateaus and setbacks along the way. However, she applied problem-solving by seeking advice from fitness experts, adjusting her workout routine, and addressing emotional eating habits. Her persistence paid off, and she not only achieved her fitness goals but also developed resilience in the process.

Goal Achievement as Resilience Building

Confidence: Successfully achieving goals through problem-solving enhances your confidence in your abilities to overcome challenges.

Persistence: The resilience developed during problem-solving helps you persist in the face of setbacks and obstacles.

Adaptability: Problem-solving equips you with the skills to adapt to changing circumstances, which is crucial in goal pursuit.

Conclusion: Achieving Goals and Building Resilience

Problem-solving is a powerful tool that can bridge the gap between setting goals and achieving them. By applying structured problem-solving techniques, you not only move closer to your goals but also cultivate resilience along the way. In the chapters that follow, we will continue to explore how problem-solving can be applied to various aspects of life to promote mental well-being and personal growth.

Step 8: The Resilience Mindset

As we conclude this chapter, we'll reflect on the resilience mindset. We'll understand that resilience isn't a destination; it's a way of life. Through problem-solving, we can embrace resilience as an ongoing journey, a commitment to growth, and a steadfast approach to life's challenges. We'll also appreciate that stress is not a foe but a companion on this journey, guiding us toward greater resilience through effective problem-solving.

Embracing Resilience as a Way of Life

Continuous Growth: Resilience is not a static trait; it's a dynamic skill that evolves over time. Embrace the idea that you can continually enhance your resilience through practice and learning.

Adopting a Solution-Oriented Mindset: The resilience mindset is inherently solution-oriented. It's the belief that every problem you encounter is an opportunity for growth and learning.

Stress as a Companion: Rather than viewing stress as an enemy, see it as a companion on your resilience journey. Stress can guide you toward areas where you need to build resilience.

Resilience in Action

Adapting to Change: Embrace change as a chance to exercise your resilience muscle. Whether it's a new job, a move to a different city, or a shift in personal circumstances, approach it with a problem-solving mindset.

Navigating Relationships: Use problem-solving to address conflicts and challenges in relationships. Communication, empathy, and compromise are tools in your resilience toolkit.

Pursuing Goals: Set ambitious goals and tackle them with determination. Understand that the journey may be fraught with obstacles, but each obstacle is an opportunity to enhance your resilience.

Conclusion: The Resilience Journey

Resilience isn't about avoiding stress or challenges; it's about facing them head-on with a problem-solving mindset. It's a journey of growth, learning, and self-discovery. By cultivating resilience through problem-solving, you equip yourself to thrive in the face of adversity and emerge stronger from life's challenges. In the chapters that follow, we will continue to explore how problem-solving can be applied to various aspects of life to promote mental well-being and personal growth.

By the end of Chapter 3, we will have unveiled the powerful connection between stress, resilience, and problem-solving. We'll have acquired practical strategies for reducing stress and building resilience through problem-solving. Armed with this knowledge, we'll be better equipped to navigate life's complexities with poise, adaptability, and a resilient spirit, ultimately leading us toward greater personal growth and mental well-being.

Chapter 4: Empowerment through Problem-Solving: Taking Control of Your Journey

Section 1: The Path to Empowerment

In this chapter, we delve into the empowering aspects of problem-solving. We'll explore how the process of finding solutions can transform us into active agents of change, fostering self-confidence and a deep belief in our abilities.

Step 1: Empowerment: A Catalyst for Change

Empowerment isn't a passive state; it's a catalyst for transformation. In this step, we'll examine the concept of empowerment and its role in our personal growth and mental well-being. We'll understand how effective problem-solving can empower us to take control of our lives, make decisions with confidence, and shape our destinies.

Empowerment: The Key to Personal Transformation

Defining Empowerment: We'll start by defining empowerment and recognizing it as a dynamic force that propels us toward positive change. Empowerment is not merely about external control but about an internal sense of mastery and self-efficacy.

The Problem-Solving Connection: Explore how problem-solving serves as a vehicle for empowerment. It empowers us to confront challenges head-on, transforming them from roadblocks into stepping stones.

Taking Control: Understand that empowerment involves taking control of our lives. Problem-solving equips us with the tools to make informed decisions and actively shape our circumstances.

Confidence Through Problem-Solving

Confidence Building: Effective problem-solving enhances our confidence. When we successfully solve problems, we gain a sense of accomplishment and self-assurance.

Decision-Making: Empowerment is closely linked to the ability to make decisions with confidence. Problem-solving helps us analyze options and choose the best course of action.

Personal Growth and Empowerment

Resilience: Empowerment fosters resilience. When we feel in control of our lives and capable of finding solutions, we are better equipped to bounce back from setbacks.

Continuous Learning: Problem-solving encourages continuous learning and growth. Every challenge we face becomes an opportunity for personal development.

Empowerment as a Lifelong Journey

Mindset Shift: Embrace the idea that empowerment is an ongoing journey, not a destination. It's a commitment to continuous growth and self-improvement.

Problem-Solving as an Empowerment Tool: Recognize the value of problem-solving as a tool for empowerment. As we explore problem-solving techniques and strategies in this book, we'll equip ourselves with the means to become active agents of change in our lives.

Conclusion: The Empowerment-Problem-Solving Connection

Empowerment is the driving force behind personal growth and mental well-being. Problem-solving is the tool that empowers us to take control, make confident decisions, and transform challenges into opportunities. As we embark on this journey of empowerment through problem-solving, we lay the foundation for a more empowered and fulfilling life.

Step 2: Problem-Solving as a Vehicle for Empowerment

Problem-solving is not just about finding answers; it's about gaining agency over our circumstances. In this step, we'll delve into how the process of finding solutions can empower us. Through real-life examples and exercises, we'll uncover how effective problem-solving empowers us to become proactive, self-reliant, and resilient individuals.

The Empowerment Within Problem-Solving

Taking Initiative: Problem-solving encourages us to take the initiative. Instead of waiting for problems to resolve themselves, we become proactive in seeking solutions.

Self-Reliance: As we learn to solve problems, we become less dependent on external sources for solutions. This self-reliance is a key aspect of empowerment.

Resilience: Problem-solving equips us to bounce back from setbacks and adapt to changing circumstances. This resilience is a result of our empowerment to face challenges head-on.

Real-Life Examples of Empowerment through Problem-Solving

Financial Empowerment: Sarah faced financial difficulties but empowered herself through effective budgeting and financial planning.

She learned to take control of her finances, reducing stress and gaining a sense of security.

Career Advancement: John sought career advancement and empowered himself by developing new skills through online courses and networking. He applied problem-solving techniques to navigate office politics and advance in his career.

Exercises to Enhance Empowerment through Problem-Solving

Personal Challenge Journal: Maintain a journal where you document personal challenges you face and how you address them. Reflect on your feelings of empowerment as you overcome each obstacle.

Skills Enhancement: Identify a skill or knowledge gap that you believe would empower you in your personal or professional life. Take concrete steps to acquire or enhance that skill through courses, workshops, or self-study.

Resilience Building: When facing adversity, apply problem-solving skills to address the situation rather than feeling helpless. Document your problem-solving process and note how it empowers you to navigate difficulties.

Problem-Solving as a Mindset of Empowerment

A Shift in Perspective: Understand that problem-solving is not just a series of steps but a mindset of empowerment. Embrace it as a way of taking control over your life and shaping your destiny.

The Continuous Journey: Recognize that empowerment through problem-solving is a lifelong journey. Each problem you encounter is an opportunity to strengthen your sense of agency and resilience.

Conclusion: Embracing Empowerment through Problem-Solving

Problem-solving is a powerful vehicle for empowerment, enabling us to take control, become self-reliant, and bounce back from challenges. As we continue to explore problem-solving techniques and strategies, we equip ourselves with the tools to be proactive, confident, and resilient individuals. In this journey, empowerment becomes not just a concept but a tangible force for personal growth and well-being.

Section 2: Developing Empowering Problem-Solving Skills

Step 3: The Role of Decision-Making

Decision-making is at the core of empowerment. In this step, we'll explore the connection between problem-solving and decision-making. We'll learn how to make informed decisions by gathering data, weighing options, and considering consequences. Through decision-making exercises, we'll enhance our ability to make choices that empower us on our journey.

The Intersection of Decision-Making and Problem-Solving

Informed Choices: Decision-making is about making choices, and effective problem-solving provides us with the information and options needed to make informed decisions.

Confidence Building: As we become better decision-makers, our confidence in our problem-solving abilities grows. This confidence is a source of empowerment.

Ownership: Decision-making gives us ownership over our choices. When we actively participate in making decisions, we feel more empowered to handle the outcomes.

Making Empowering Decisions

Gathering Information: We'll explore how to gather relevant information when facing a decision. This includes seeking data, consulting experts, and conducting research.

Weighing Options: Decision-making involves evaluating different options. We'll learn techniques to weigh the pros and cons of each choice effectively.

Considering Consequences: Part of empowerment is understanding the potential consequences of our decisions. We'll delve into methods for forecasting the outcomes of our choices.

Decision-Making Exercises for Empowerment

The Decision Journal: Keep a decision journal where you record significant decisions you make. Reflect on the process, the factors you considered, and the outcomes. This helps you refine your decision-making skills.

Role Play: Practice decision-making through role-playing scenarios where you have to make choices. This allows you to experiment with different decision-making approaches in a safe environment.

Consultation: Seek advice from trusted friends, mentors, or colleagues when facing important decisions. Learn from their perspectives and incorporate their insights into your decision-making process.

Empowerment Through Responsible Decision-Making

Ownership of Outcomes: Understand that empowerment also means taking responsibility for the outcomes of your decisions, whether they are positive or challenging.

Learning from Decisions: Every decision is a learning opportunity. Use the feedback from your choices to refine your decision-making skills and become a more empowered decision-maker.

Conclusion: Empowerment through Informed Decision-Making

Empowerment is closely tied to our ability to make informed decisions. By integrating problem-solving and decision-making, we not only become better equipped to address challenges but also gain a sense of control over our lives. As we continue on this journey of developing empowering problem-solving skills, we'll find that the ability to make wise choices is a powerful source of empowerment and personal growth.

Step 4: Confidence Building through Problem-Solving

Self-confidence is the cornerstone of empowerment. In this step, we'll delve into how problem-solving can boost our confidence. We'll discover how each successfully solved problem becomes a building block of self-assurance. Through practical exercises, we'll develop greater confidence in our problem-solving abilities.

The Role of Confidence in Empowerment

Self-Belief: Confidence is rooted in self-belief. When we believe in our ability to tackle challenges and find solutions, we are more likely to take action.

Empowerment Catalyst: Confidence is a catalyst for empowerment. It enables us to step out of our comfort zones, make decisions, and take control of our lives.

Resilience Booster: Confident individuals are better equipped to bounce back from setbacks. They view obstacles as opportunities to apply their problem-solving skills.

Building Confidence through Problem-Solving

Success Stories: We'll explore real-life success stories of individuals who overcame challenges through effective problem-solving. These stories illustrate how each solved problem contributes to greater self-confidence.

Competence and Mastery: As we become more adept at problem-solving, we gain a sense of competence and mastery. This, in turn, enhances our confidence.

Mindset Shift: We'll shift our mindset from self-doubt to self-assurance. Embracing the idea that we can solve problems empowers us to approach challenges with confidence.

Practical Exercises for Confidence Building

Problem-Solving Challenges: Engage in problem-solving challenges, both small and large. Document your successes and celebrate them as victories that boost your confidence.

Positive Self-Talk: Practice positive self-talk and affirmations that reinforce your belief in your problem-solving abilities. Replace self-doubt with self-encouragement.

Visualization: Visualize yourself confidently addressing and solving problems. This mental rehearsal can enhance your actual problem-solving performance.

Confidence as a Lifelong Skill

Continuous Improvement: Understand that confidence, like problem-solving, is a skill that can be continuously improved. Each problem you solve contributes to your self-assurance.

Failure as a Stepping Stone: Embrace failures as stepping stones to greater confidence. Each setback is an opportunity to learn and grow, ultimately making you a more empowered individual.

Conclusion: Confidence as the Key to Empowerment

Confidence is not a fixed trait but a dynamic skill that can be cultivated through problem-solving. As we continue to develop our confidence in our problem-solving abilities, we become more empowered to tackle challenges, make decisions, and shape our destinies. This journey of empowerment through confidence is an integral part of our overall personal growth and well-being.

Section 3: The Journey to Self-Belief

Step 5: Problem-Solving and Self-Belief

Self-belief is the engine that drives us toward personal growth and mental well-being. In this step, we'll explore how problem-solving nurtures self-belief. We'll learn to overcome self-doubt by recognizing our capacity to find solutions. Through affirmations and mindset shifts, we'll cultivate a deep belief in our abilities.

The Power of Self-Belief

Self-Belief Defined: We'll start by defining self-belief as the unwavering belief in one's own capabilities and potential. It's the foundation upon which empowerment is built.

The Role of Self-Belief: Understand that self-belief is a driving force behind personal growth and resilience. It fuels our motivation to tackle challenges and navigate life's complexities.

Problem-Solving as a Self-Belief Booster

Recognizing Our Capabilities: Problem-solving helps us recognize our capabilities. Each successfully solved problem reinforces the idea that we have the competence to address challenges.

Overcoming Self-Doubt: Self-doubt is a common hurdle. We'll explore how problem-solving can help us overcome self-doubt by providing evidence of our abilities.

Mindset Shift: Shift our mindset from "I can't" to "I can." Problem-solving becomes a tool to challenge and reshape limiting beliefs.

Cultivating Self-Belief through Problem-Solving

Positive Affirmations: Practice positive affirmations that reinforce your belief in your problem-solving abilities. Use statements like "I am a capable problem solver" to boost your self-belief.

Visualization: Visualize yourself confidently and successfully solving problems. This mental imagery can strengthen your self-belief.

Goal Setting: Set challenging but achievable problem-solving goals. As you achieve these goals, your self-belief grows.

Self-Belief as a Lifelong Journey

Embracing Challenges: Understand that challenges are opportunities to nurture self-belief. Embrace them as chances to prove your capabilities.

Continuous Growth: Self-belief, like problem-solving, is not static. It grows and evolves with each problem you solve and each obstacle you overcome.

Conclusion: Self-Belief as a Catalyst for Empowerment

Self-belief is a fundamental element of empowerment, and problem-solving is a powerful tool for cultivating it. As we continue on this journey of self-belief through problem-solving, we not only become more confident individuals but also more resilient and empowered to shape our destinies. Self-belief becomes the catalyst that propels us toward personal growth and mental well-being.

Step 6: Problem-Solving and Independence

Independence is a natural byproduct of empowerment. In this step, we'll delve into how problem-solving fosters independence. We'll learn to rely on our problem-solving skills to navigate life's challenges autonomously. Through exercises in self-reliance, we'll embrace independence as a path to personal growth and mental well-being.

The Link Between Independence and Empowerment

Independence Defined: Start by defining independence as the ability to make decisions and take actions without undue reliance on others. It's a key aspect of empowerment.

Empowerment through Independence: Understand that independence is closely linked to empowerment. When we can address challenges independently, we feel more in control of our lives.

Problem-Solving as a Path to Independence

Taking Initiative: Problem-solving encourages us to take initiative when we face challenges. This proactive approach fosters a sense of self-reliance.

Autonomy in Decision-Making: As we become more adept problem solvers, we gain autonomy in making decisions. We rely less on external guidance.

Navigating Life's Labyrinth: Problem-solving equips us with the skills to navigate the complexities of life independently. We develop a resourceful mindset.

Exercises in Self-Reliance

Solo Problem-Solving Challenges: Engage in problem-solving challenges where you deliberately tackle problems on your own, without seeking immediate assistance. Reflect on what you learn from these experiences.

Personal Projects: Undertake personal projects that require problem-solving, whether it's planning a trip, managing finances, or learning a new skill. This builds your sense of independence.

Seek Guidance Thoughtfully: When facing complex challenges, practice seeking guidance thoughtfully. Instead of relying entirely on others, use guidance as a supplement to your problem-solving efforts.

Independence as a Mindset

Shift in Perspective: Embrace independence as a mindset. View it as a source of strength and a means to personal growth.

Embracing Self-Reliance: Recognize that self-reliance is not about isolation but about being capable and resourceful. It's a sign of personal strength.

Independence as a Lifelong Journey

Continuous Learning: Understand that independence, like problem-solving, is a skill that can be honed throughout life. Every challenge you address independently contributes to your growth.

Interdependence: Acknowledge that while independence is valuable, interdependence is also essential. Balance self-reliance with collaboration and support from others when needed.

Conclusion: Independence as a Path to Empowerment

Independence is a vital component of empowerment, and problem-solving is the tool that fosters it. As we continue to develop our independence through problem-solving, we not only become more self-reliant individuals but also more empowered to tackle life's challenges. Independence becomes a path to personal growth, mental well-being, and a deeper sense of empowerment.

Section 4: Applying Empowerment to Life's Challenges

Step 7: Empowerment in Everyday Life

Empowerment isn't an abstract concept; it's a way of approaching daily challenges. In this step, we'll explore how to apply the principles of empowerment through problem-solving in our everyday lives. We'll learn to see each obstacle as an opportunity for empowerment, self-belief, and personal growth.

Bringing Empowerment into Daily Life

Everyday Empowerment Defined: We'll begin by defining what everyday empowerment means. It's the practice of applying the principles of self-belief, independence, and confidence to address daily challenges.

Empowerment Mindset: Understand that an empowerment mindset is not reserved for major life events. It can be woven into the fabric of our daily lives.

Empowering Approaches to Everyday Challenges

Routine Problem-Solving: Incorporate problem-solving into your daily routines. For example, use decision-making skills to plan meals or manage your schedule effectively.

Communication: Apply empowerment principles in communication. Speak assertively, express your needs, and solve communication challenges proactively.

Time Management: Use problem-solving skills to manage your time efficiently. Prioritize tasks, set goals, and make informed choices about how you spend your time.

Seeing Obstacles as Opportunities

Perspective Shift: Shift your perspective on obstacles. Instead of viewing them as barriers, see them as opportunities to practice problem-solving, build self-belief, and demonstrate independence.

Learning and Growth: Understand that everyday challenges offer valuable lessons and opportunities for personal growth. Each obstacle can be a stepping stone toward greater empowerment.

Exercises in Everyday Empowerment

Daily Problem-Solving Journal: Maintain a journal where you document everyday challenges you face and how you apply problem-solving and empowerment principles to address them.

Reflect and Learn: Regularly reflect on how you've applied empowerment in your daily life. Identify areas where you've grown in confidence, independence, and self-belief.

Empowerment as a Lifestyle

Consistency: Embrace everyday empowerment as a lifestyle. Consistently applying these principles in small ways leads to significant personal growth over time.

A Path to Fulfillment: Recognize that living an empowered life is not just about solving problems but also about finding fulfillment, meaning, and satisfaction in your daily experiences.

Conclusion: Everyday Empowerment for Personal Growth

Empowerment is not limited to grand gestures or major life events; it's a way of approaching daily challenges. By applying the principles of self-belief, independence, and confidence through problem-solving in our everyday lives, we not only become more empowered individuals but also experience continuous personal growth and enhanced well-being. Everyday empowerment becomes a path to a more fulfilling and satisfying life.

Step 8: The Empowered Mindset

As we conclude this chapter, we'll reflect on the empowered mindset. We'll understand that empowerment isn't a destination; it's an ongoing journey. Through problem-solving, we embrace empowerment as a way of life, a commitment to taking control of our destinies, and a steadfast approach to life's challenges.

The Empowerment Mindset Defined

Empowerment as a Journey: We'll begin by defining the empowerment mindset as an ongoing journey, not a static state. It's a commitment to continuous growth and self-improvement.

Problem-Solving as a Lifestyle: Understand that problem-solving is the vehicle through which we practice and embrace this empowerment mindset in our daily lives.

Embracing Empowerment as a Way of Life

A Commitment to Growth: Recognize that empowerment is about continuous personal growth. Each problem we solve, each challenge we face, is an opportunity to grow.

A Steadfast Approach: Embrace an unwavering approach to life's challenges. Regardless of the size or complexity of the obstacle, you approach it with the confidence that you have the tools to address it.

Empowerment as a Personal Commitment

Ownership of Choices: Understand that empowerment involves taking ownership of your choices and decisions. You actively shape your destiny.

Resilience Building: Realize that an empowered mindset fosters resilience. It enables you to bounce back from setbacks, using each challenge as a stepping stone toward personal growth.

Problem-Solving as the Path to Empowerment

Problem-Solving as a Skill: Understand that problem-solving is not just a means to an end; it's a skill that empowers us to approach life's challenges with confidence and self-assurance.

A Continuous Journey: Embrace the idea that empowerment through problem-solving is a lifelong journey. It's not a destination but a way of life.

Conclusion: The Empowerment Mindset as a Lifelong Journey

Empowerment is not a final destination; it's an ongoing journey. Through problem-solving, we cultivate an empowered mindset that guides us in taking control of our destinies, facing life's challenges with confidence, and committing to continuous growth and self-improvement. As we move forward in this book, we carry with us the understanding that empowerment is not just a concept but a tangible force for personal growth, mental well-being, and a more fulfilling life.

By the end of Chapter 4, we will have journeyed through the transformative power of empowerment through problem-solving. We'll have acquired practical skills to make informed decisions, build confidence, nurture self-belief, and cultivate independence. Armed with this empowerment, we'll be better equipped to approach life's challenges with confidence and resilience, ultimately leading us toward greater personal growth and mental well-being. This chapter has provided us with the tools and mindset needed to navigate the complexities of life with a proactive and empowered outlook, allowing us to thrive in the face of adversity and continuously evolve as individuals. As we move forward in this book, we carry with us the conviction that empowerment through problem-solving is not just a theory but a practical path to a more fulfilling and enriched life.

"Success usually comes to those who are too busy to be looking for it." — Henry David

Thoreau

Chapter 5: Mastering the Art of Problem Solving

Section 1: Identifying and Defining the Problem

In the journey to becoming a proficient problem solver, the first crucial step is to learn how to identify and define the problem accurately. This is where the process begins, and the foundation of your problem-solving endeavor takes shape.

Step 1: Identify the Problem

Imagine a ship navigating through treacherous waters. Before charting a course or making any decisions, the captain must first identify the hazards, obstacles, and potential dangers lurking beneath the surface. Similarly, in problem-solving, identifying the problem is akin to recognizing the obstacles that lie ahead.

To identify the problem effectively:

• Ask the Right Questions: Start by asking questions to gain a clear understanding of what you are dealing with. What is the root cause of the issue? What are the symptoms or manifestations of the problem? Who is affected by it?

• Gather Information: Gather all relevant data and information that pertain to the problem. This could involve researching, conducting surveys, or consulting with subject matter experts. The more you know about the problem, the better equipped you are to address it.

Problem-solving is a skill that empowers us in various aspects of life. In this chapter, we embark on a journey to master the art of problem-solving. It all starts with the crucial first step: identifying the problem.

The Significance of Problem Identification

Clarity and Precision: Understand that identifying the problem with clarity and precision is the foundation of effective problem-solving. Without a clear understanding of what needs to be addressed, finding a solution becomes challenging.

Targeted Efforts: Identifying the problem narrows down your focus. It allows you to direct your problem-solving efforts efficiently, saving time and resources.

The Process of Problem Identification

Observation and Awareness: Learn to be observant and aware of your surroundings and circumstances. Often, problems reveal themselves through subtle signs and signals.

Active Listening: When dealing with interpersonal or communication-related issues, active listening can help identify the underlying problems or conflicts.

Questioning: Ask questions to delve deeper into the issue. Use techniques like the "Five Whys" to uncover the root causes of problems.

The Importance of Framing

Framing the Problem: Understand that how you frame a problem can significantly impact the solutions you generate. We'll explore different approaches to framing problems effectively.

Practical Exercises for Problem Identification

Problem Journal: Maintain a problem journal where you record issues you encounter daily. Describe the problem, its context, and any initial observations.

Problem-Spotting Challenge: Engage in a problem-spotting challenge where you actively seek out problems in your environment. This exercise enhances your problem awareness.

Ask for Feedback: When faced with a challenge, seek feedback from colleagues, mentors, or friends. They may offer fresh perspectives on the issue.

Conclusion: The First Step to Mastery

Identifying the problem is the first step in mastering the art of problem-solving. With this skill, you'll be better prepared to tackle a wide range of challenges effectively. As we continue in this chapter, we'll delve deeper into the process of defining problems with precision, setting the stage for innovative and effective solutions.

Step 2: Define the Problem

Once the problem is identified, the next step is to define it. This involves articulating the problem statement in a concise and precise manner. Think of it as setting the coordinates on your navigational chart, guiding you toward a solution.

To define the problem effectively:

• Be Specific: Avoid vague or ambiguous descriptions. The problem statement should be clear and specific, leaving no room for misinterpretation.

- State the Scope: Define the boundaries of the problem. What is included and what is not? Understanding the scope prevents you from tackling unrelated issues.

- Consider Constraints: Are there any limitations or constraints that need to be taken into account? These could be financial, time-related, or resource-based.

Mastering the art of identifying and defining the problem sets the stage for the problem-solving process. It's the critical first step that ensures you're navigating in the right direction.

Section 2: Generating Creative Solutions

With a clear understanding of the problem, you're now ready to dive into the creative process of generating potential solutions. This is where innovation and imagination come into play.

Step 3: Generate Alternative Solutions

Think of this step as brainstorming. The objective is to cast a wide net, exploring various ideas and approaches to solving the problem. Much like a painter with a palette of colors, you have a toolbox of ideas to choose from.

To generate alternative solutions effectively:

•   Encourage Creativity: Set aside preconceived notions and let your creativity flow. Think outside the box and consider unconventional approaches.

•   Quantity Over Quality: At this stage, prioritize quantity. Aim to generate as many ideas as possible without initially evaluating their feasibility.

•   Diverse Perspectives: Involve others in the brainstorming process. Different perspectives can lead to a broader range of ideas.

This book aims to provide readers with a comprehensive guide to mastering problem-solving skills, equipping them with the tools and mindset needed to tackle challenges effectively. As you embark on this journey, remember that problem-solving is both an art and a science, and with practice, dedication, and the right techniques, you can become a skilled problem solver in any area of your life.

Section 3: Evaluating and Choosing the Best Solution

Generating alternative solutions is just the beginning of the problem-solving journey. In this section, we explore the critical process of evaluating and selecting the most suitable solution to address the identified problem.

Step 4: Evaluate Each Solution

Imagine you have a collection of potential puzzle pieces. The next step is to carefully examine each piece to determine how well it fits into the overall picture. Similarly, during the problem-solving process, evaluating each solution involves assessing its feasibility, impact, and potential drawbacks.

To evaluate solutions effectively:

• Pros and Cons Analysis: Create a list of the advantages and disadvantages of each solution. Consider factors such as cost, time, resources, and potential risks.

- Feasibility: Assess whether each solution is practical and achievable within the given constraints. Will it work in the real world, and can it be implemented successfully?

- Alignment with Goals: Ensure that the chosen solution aligns with your overall objectives. Does it address the root cause of the problem, or is it merely a temporary fix?

Step 5: Choose the Best Solution

The goal of evaluation is to identify the most promising solution. This is the puzzle piece that not only fits but also contributes significantly to solving the problem. Like a curator selecting the finest artwork for an exhibition, your role is to choose the solution that stands out from the rest.

To choose the best solution effectively:

- Consider Trade-offs: Recognize that no solution is perfect. Be prepared to make trade-offs and prioritize what matters most in your specific context.

• Stakeholder Input: If applicable, gather input from relevant stakeholders. Their perspectives can provide valuable insights and increase buy-in for the chosen solution.

• Long-Term Vision: Think beyond the immediate problem. Consider the long-term implications and sustainability of the chosen solution.

By the end of this step, you should have a well-defined, feasible solution that you are confident will address the problem at hand.

Section 4: Implementation and Continuous Improvement

With the chosen solution in hand, it's time to roll up your sleeves and put your problem-solving plan into action. However, the process doesn't end here. Continuous improvement and adaptation are key to long-term success.

Step 6: Develop an Action Plan

An action plan is your roadmap for implementing the chosen solution. It outlines the specific steps, responsibilities, timelines, and resources needed to bring your solution to life. Think of it as the blueprint for constructing a solution to your problem.

To develop an action plan effectively:

• Break it Down: Divide the plan into manageable tasks and subtasks. This makes progress more measurable and achievable.

• Set Milestones: Establish milestones or checkpoints to track progress. Celebrate small victories along the way.

• Assign Responsibilities: Clearly define who is responsible for each task. Accountability ensures that progress continues smoothly.

Step 7: Implement the Solution

Putting your action plan into action is where the rubber meets the road. Execute the planned steps, monitor progress, and make necessary adjustments as you work toward solving the problem.

To implement the solution effectively:

• Stay Flexible: Be prepared to adapt to unforeseen challenges or changes in circumstances. Flexibility is key to successful implementation.

- Communication: Keep stakeholders informed about progress and any changes to the plan. Effective communication helps maintain support and buy-in. "Think of stakeholders as the folks who have some skin in the game, the ones who care about what's happening and how it affects them. They're like the VIPs of the situation, whether it's a project, a company, or even a community event. Stakeholders can be anyone from the big shots running the show to the regular folks living next door. They all have something at stake, something they're invested in – be it money, time, or just their general well-being."

Step 8: Adapt and Adjust

Problem-solving is a dynamic process. As you implement your solution, be open to adjustments and modifications. Sometimes, new information or unexpected obstacles require you to adapt your approach.

To adapt and adjust effectively:

- Learn from Mistakes: View setbacks as opportunities for learning and improvement. Analyze what went wrong and how you can do better next time.

- Feedback Loop: Establish a feedback loop with stakeholders and team members. Encourage open communication to identify areas for improvement.

This chapter offers a comprehensive guide to mastering the art of problem solving. It takes you through the intricate steps of identifying, defining, generating, evaluating, choosing, developing an action plan, implementing, and adapting solutions. The journey of becoming a skilled problem solver is not a destination but a continuous process of growth and refinement. As you apply these principles in your life, you'll find yourself better equipped to face and conquer a wide range of challenges, both big and small.

Stay curious, stay determined, and embrace problem solving as a lifelong skill that empowers you to navigate the complexities of the world with confidence.

Section 5: Evaluating the Outcome and Continuous Learning

As you progress through the implementation phase of your problem-solving journey, it's crucial to maintain a vigilant eye on the outcomes and continuously seek opportunities for improvement. This section delves into the importance of evaluating the results and the ongoing process of learning and refinement.

Step 9: Evaluate the Outcome

With the solution implemented, it's time to assess its impact on the problem you set out to solve. Evaluating the outcome provides valuable insights into the effectiveness of your chosen solution and helps you make informed decisions for the future.

To evaluate the outcome effectively:

• Measure Against Goals: Compare the actual results with the goals and objectives you established during the problem-solving process. Did you achieve what you set out to do?

• Collect Feedback: Seek feedback from stakeholders, team members, and those directly affected by the solution. Their perspectives can reveal aspects you might have overlooked.

• Quantitative and Qualitative Data: Use both quantitative data (numbers, metrics) and qualitative data (observations, feedback) to gain a comprehensive understanding of the outcome.

Step 10: Learn and Iterate

Problem-solving is a dynamic process, and the insights gained from evaluating outcomes are invaluable for your growth as a problem solver. Learning from both your successes and failures is central to continuous improvement.

To learn and iterate effectively:

• Reflect on the Process: Analyze the entire problem-solving process, from identification to implementation. Identify what worked well and what could be improved.

• Document Lessons: Keep a record of lessons learned. Documenting your experiences and insights creates a knowledge base that you can draw upon in future challenges.

• Apply Feedback: Use the feedback received during the evaluation process to inform your approach in future problem-solving endeavors.

By embracing the principle of continuous learning, you not only refine your problem-solving skills but also position yourself as a proactive and adaptable individual in various aspects of life.

Section 6: Seeking Guidance and Building Expertise

Problem-solving is a skill that can always be honed, and seeking guidance from experts and mentors can accelerate your growth as a problem solver.

Step 11: Seek Guidance

The wisdom of others who have faced similar challenges or have expertise in specific domains can be a valuable resource. Don't hesitate to seek guidance when confronting complex problems.

To seek guidance effectively:

• Identify Mentors: Look for individuals who excel in problem-solving within your field of interest. Approach them for mentorship and insights.

• Networking: Attend workshops, seminars, and conferences related to your area of interest. Networking can connect you with experienced problem solvers.

• Online Resources: Utilize online forums, courses, and communities dedicated to problem-solving. The internet offers a wealth of knowledge and connections.

Step 12: Build Expertise

Expertise in problem-solving is cultivated over time through practice and continuous learning. As you confront and solve a diverse range of problems, you naturally become more adept.

To build expertise effectively:

• Diverse Challenges: Seek out diverse challenges, both professionally and personally. The more varied your problem-solving experiences, the more versatile your skills become.

• Share Knowledge: Teach others what you've learned. Teaching reinforces your own understanding and positions you as an expert in your field.

• Stay Inquisitive: Maintain a curious mindset. Ask questions, explore new ideas, and stay up-to-date with developments in your areas of interest.

This chapter has explored the intricacies of problem-solving, from its inception to the ongoing process of evaluation, learning, and expertise development. By mastering this art, you're not only equipping yourself to navigate life's challenges but also positioning yourself as a valuable problem solver in your personal and professional circles.

As you progress on your journey, remember that problem-solving is not a one-time task but a continuous way of approaching life. Embrace it with enthusiasm and determination, and you'll find yourself more capable and confident in the face of any problem that comes your way.

Section 7: Embracing Problem-Solving as a Way of Life

As you journey through the various steps and stages of problem solving, it's essential to recognize that this skill can transcend individual challenges. It can become an integral part of your life, shaping your approach to not just problems, but opportunities as well. In this section, we explore the mindset and lifestyle of a proficient problem solver.

Step 13: Stay Curious and Inquisitive

At the heart of effective problem solving lies curiosity. This innate human trait has propelled us forward through centuries of discovery and innovation. Cultivating your curiosity and inquisitiveness is key to being an adept problem solver.

To stay curious and inquisitive effectively:

• Ask "Why?": Don't be content with superficial answers. Dig deeper by asking "why" to uncover root causes and hidden connections.

• Explore New Perspectives: Seek out diverse viewpoints and perspectives. Engage in conversations with people from different backgrounds and experiences.

• Continuous Learning: Embrace learning as a lifelong endeavor. Dedicate time to acquiring new knowledge and skills regularly.

Step 14: Embrace Failure as a Learning Opportunity

Failure is not the end but a stepping stone to success. Every setback, every mistake, offers a valuable lesson. Embracing failure as part of the journey is a hallmark of a resilient problem solver.

To embrace failure as a learning opportunity effectively:

- Shift Your Mindset: See failure not as a reflection of your abilities but as a temporary setback. It's an opportunity to refine your approach.

- Analyze Mistakes: After facing a setback, take the time to analyze what went wrong. Identify areas for improvement and implement changes.

- Share Your Experiences: Don't be afraid to share your failures and the lessons learned with others. It not only helps you but also supports a culture of growth and learning.

Step 15: Seek Opportunities for Growth

Every challenge, no matter how daunting, holds the potential for personal and professional growth. Problem solving becomes a way of life when you actively seek opportunities for growth in every situation.

To seek opportunities for growth effectively:

- Step Out of Your Comfort Zone: Don't shy away from challenges simply because they seem difficult. The greatest growth often occurs outside your comfort zone.

- Set Goals: Establish personal and professional goals that require problem-solving skills to achieve. Striving toward these goals keeps you engaged and motivated.

- Reflect and Adapt: Regularly reflect on your experiences and adapt your approach. Learning from your successes and failures is the path to continuous improvement.

In this section, we've explored the mindset and lifestyle of a proficient problem solver. By embracing curiosity, learning from failure, and seeking opportunities for growth, you not only become a more effective problem solver but also set yourself on a path of personal development and lifelong fulfillment.

Problem solving, when approached with the right attitude and techniques, becomes more than just a tool; it becomes a philosophy for navigating the complexities of life with resilience and purpose.

Section 8: Inspiring Others and Leaving a Legacy

The journey of becoming a skilled problem solver not only benefits you personally but can also inspire and impact those around you. In this section, we explore the profound influence of problem-solving skills on others and the idea of leaving a lasting legacy.

Step 16: Inspiring Others

As you navigate life's challenges with grace and competence, you become a source of inspiration for others. Your problem-solving journey can motivate and empower those in your sphere of influence to tackle their own difficulties with confidence.

To inspire others effectively:

• Lead by Example: Demonstrate the problem-solving mindset in action. Your actions speak louder than words, and others will follow suit when they see your approach.

• Share Your Stories: Share your experiences, both successes, and failures, openly. Personal anecdotes can be powerful tools for inspiring and connecting with others.

• Offer Guidance: Be willing to mentor or guide others who seek your advice or insights. Your expertise can help them navigate their own challenges.

Step 17: Leaving a Legacy

Effective problem solvers have the potential to leave a lasting legacy not only through their accomplishments but also through the impact they have on the world. Leaving a legacy means making a meaningful and enduring contribution to society.

To leave a legacy effectively:

• Define Your Values: Clarify your core values and principles. Your legacy should align with these values and reflect what matters most to you.

• Contribute to a Cause: Consider how your problem-solving skills can benefit causes or organizations you are passionate about. Volunteering your expertise can leave a lasting impact.

• Teach and Share Knowledge: Passing on your problem-solving knowledge through teaching, writing, or mentoring ensures that your wisdom lives on through others.

Section 9: The Lifelong Journey of Problem Solving

> In this final section, we reflect on the lifelong nature of problem solving. It's not just a skill to be acquired but a journey to be embraced with enthusiasm and dedication.

Step 18: Embrace Problem-Solving as a Way of Life

Problem-solving is not a finite task with a defined end; it's a continuous journey. Embrace it as a way of life, and you'll find yourself better equipped to navigate the complexities of the world with confidence and resilience.

To embrace problem-solving as a way of life effectively:

• Cultivate Resilience: Develop the mental fortitude to face challenges head-on. Understand that each problem is an opportunity for growth.

• Stay Committed: Commit to ongoing learning and improvement. Problem solving becomes more natural and effective with practice.

• Inspire Others: Encourage those around you to adopt a problem-solving mindset. Your influence can create a ripple effect of positive change.

As you conclude this chapter, remember that problem-solving is not just a skill; it's a philosophy for approaching life with curiosity, resilience, and a commitment to making a positive impact. By mastering the art of problem solving, you're not only bettering yourself but also leaving a lasting legacy of empowerment and inspiration for generations to come.

Chapter Conclusion: A Lifelong Pursuit of Mastery

This chapter has explored the depth and breadth of problem-solving skills, from its practical application in everyday challenges to its profound impact on individuals and society as a whole. The journey of mastering this art is a lifelong pursuit, one that offers not only personal fulfillment but also the opportunity to inspire and empower others.

As you embark on your own problem-solving journey, remember that each challenge is an opportunity, each failure a stepping stone, and each success a testament to your growth. Embrace the journey with enthusiasm, for it is a path to becoming a more capable, resilient, and impactful individual.

Chapter 6: Building Self-Confidence and Overcoming Fear through Problem Solving

In this chapter, we'll explore how the art of problem-solving can be a powerful tool in building self-confidence and conquering fear. Self-confidence and the ability to face our fears head-on are vital components of mental well-being and personal growth. By understanding the role of problem-solving in this context, you can empower yourself to become more self-assured and fearless.

Section 1: The Connection Between Problem-Solving and Self-Confidence

Step 1: Recognizing the Importance of Self-Confidence

Self-confidence is the cornerstone of mental well-being. In this step, we'll delve into why self-confidence is essential for your overall happiness and how it impacts your ability to tackle life's challenges.

Step 2: Problem-Solving as a Confidence Builder

Effective problem-solving isn't just about finding solutions; it's about believing in your ability to find those solutions. We'll explore how problem-solving can boost your self-confidence by demonstrating your competence and resourcefulness.

Section 2: Overcoming Fear with Problem-Solving

Step 3: Understanding Fear and Its Impact

Fear can be a formidable barrier to personal growth and mental well-being. In this step, we'll examine the various forms of fear and how they can hold you back from reaching your full potential.

Fear's Influence on Problem-Solving

Identifying Fear: We'll begin by understanding that fear can manifest in various forms – fear of failure, fear of the unknown, fear of rejection, and more. Recognizing these fears is crucial in addressing them effectively.

Impact on Problem-Solving: Explore how fear can hinder your problem-solving abilities. It can lead to hesitation, avoidance of challenges, and reluctance to take risks.

Common Fears and Their Consequences

Fear of Failure: Understand how the fear of failure can paralyze decision-making and prevent you from attempting solutions.

Fear of the Unknown: Explore how the fear of the unknown can deter you from venturing into uncharted territory, limiting your problem-solving scope.

Fear of Rejection: Examine how the fear of rejection can hinder communication and collaboration, essential aspects of effective problem-solving.

Overcoming Fear through Problem-Solving

Rationalization: Learn to rationalize your fears. Understand that failure is a part of growth, the unknown is a realm of opportunity, and rejection is not a reflection of your worth.

Problem-Solving as a Fear-Reduction Tool: Realize that problem-solving can be a powerful tool for reducing fear. By breaking challenges into manageable parts and developing action plans, problems become less daunting.

Fear as an Indicator: Shift your perspective on fear. Instead of viewing it as a hindrance, see it as an indicator of areas where you can grow and improve.

Practical Exercises for Managing Fear

Fear Journal: Maintain a fear journal where you document your fears, their triggers, and their impact on your problem-solving efforts.

Fear-Setting: Similar to goal-setting, engage in fear-setting exercises where you outline your fears and explore potential solutions and their consequences.

Seeking Support: Seek support from mentors, friends, or support groups to discuss your fears openly. Often, sharing fears diminishes their hold over you.

Conclusion: Fear as a Catalyst for Growth

Understanding fear and its impact is a crucial step in overcoming it. By using problem-solving as a tool to confront and manage fear, you can unlock your full potential for personal growth and mental well-being. In the upcoming steps, we'll delve further into strategies for addressing and conquering fear, empowering you to approach challenges with confidence and resilience.

Step 4: Problem-Solving as Fear Conqueror

Problem-solving is a structured approach to facing challenges, including your fears. We'll delve into how problem-solving techniques can help you confront and overcome fear by breaking it down into manageable components.

Problem-Solving as Fear Conqueror

Fear Deconstruction: Understand that problem-solving is a methodical process of deconstructing complex issues into manageable components. Similarly, you can deconstruct fear into its constituent elements.

Analyzing Fear: Apply problem-solving techniques like critical thinking and analysis to examine your fear. What is the root cause? What are the factors contributing to it?

Breaking Fear into Components

Identify Specific Fears: Pinpoint specific fears within a broader issue. For example, if you fear public speaking, identify the specific aspects that trigger anxiety, such as speaking in front of a large audience or forgetting your lines.

Analyze Causes: Analyze the causes and triggers of your fears. What experiences or beliefs have contributed to them? This analytical approach can demystify fear.

Problem-Solving Techniques for Fear Conquering

Brainstorming: Use brainstorming techniques to generate ideas for addressing specific fears. Encourage creativity in finding solutions.

Root Cause Analysis: Apply root cause analysis to dig deeper into the origins of your fears. Understanding why you're afraid is the first step in overcoming it.

SWOT Analysis: Conduct a personal SWOT analysis (Strengths, Weaknesses, Opportunities, Threats) to evaluate your ability to confront and conquer fear.

Action Plans for Fear Conquering

Set Small Goals: Establish small, achievable goals to confront specific fears. Gradual exposure can desensitize you to fear-inducing situations.

Accountability: Share your fear-conquering goals with a trusted friend or mentor who can hold you accountable.

Fear Conquering as a Skill

Practice: Understand that overcoming fear is a skill that improves with practice. Each successful confrontation with fear builds your confidence.

Continuous Learning: Embrace the idea that fear is a natural part of life, and learning to manage it is an ongoing process. Continuously refine your fear-conquering strategies.

Conclusion: Fear Conquering through Problem-Solving

Problem-solving is not limited to addressing external challenges; it can be a powerful tool for conquering internal obstacles like fear. By breaking fear down into manageable components, analyzing its causes, and using problem-solving techniques to find solutions, you can gradually build the confidence and resilience needed to face your fears head-on. In the subsequent steps, we'll explore additional strategies and exercises to further empower you in your journey to conquer fear.

Section 3: Practical Problem-Solving for Confidence and Fearlessness

Step 5: Applying Problem-Solving to Self-Confidence Building

Building self-confidence is an ongoing journey. We'll explore practical problem-solving strategies that you can apply to boost your self-assurance and maintain it in your everyday life.

The Relationship Between Problem-Solving and Self-Confidence

Understanding Self-Confidence: We'll start by defining self-confidence as the belief in your abilities and judgments. Understand that self-confidence is essential for personal growth and mental well-being.

Impact of Self-Confidence on Problem-Solving: Explore how self-confidence can enhance your problem-solving abilities. When you believe in your capacity to find solutions, you approach challenges with a positive mindset.

Practical Problem-Solving for Self-Confidence Building

Setting Achievable Goals: Use problem-solving techniques to set achievable goals for self-improvement. Breaking down larger goals into manageable steps builds confidence.

Embracing Failure: Problem-solving can help you reframe failure as a learning opportunity. Understand that setbacks are part of the problem-solving process, not indicators of incompetence.

Positive Self-Talk: Apply problem-solving to address negative self-talk and self-doubt. Challenge irrational beliefs and replace them with rational, constructive thoughts.

Problem-Solving Strategies for Self-Confidence

SWOT Analysis: Conduct a personal SWOT analysis to assess your strengths and opportunities for self-improvement. Leveraging your strengths builds confidence.

Root Cause Analysis: Apply root cause analysis to identify the underlying causes of self-doubt or low self-esteem. Understanding the origins of these feelings is the first step in addressing them.

Daily Practices for Self-Confidence Building

Affirmations: Develop a daily practice of positive affirmations that reinforce your self-confidence. Use problem-solving to identify areas where you can affirm your abilities.

Visualizations: Use problem-solving to create mental images of your success. Visualize yourself confidently overcoming challenges and achieving your goals.

Feedback and Reflection

Feedback Loop: Establish a feedback loop for self-improvement. Regularly assess your progress and adjust your self-confidence-building strategies as needed.

Journaling: Maintain a confidence-building journal where you document your successes, challenges, and lessons learned. Problem-solving can help you reflect on these experiences.

Conclusion: Self-Confidence as a Problem-Solving Skill

Self-confidence is not a fixed trait but a skill that can be developed and enhanced through problem-solving. By applying problem-solving strategies to your self-confidence-building efforts, you empower yourself to approach challenges with a positive mindset and a belief in your abilities. As we progress in this chapter, we'll delve deeper into strategies for nurturing self-belief and cultivating independence, further enriching your journey toward personal growth and mental well-being.

Step 6: Problem-Solving Your Way to Fearlessness

Fearlessness doesn't mean the absence of fear but the ability to confront it courageously. In this step, we'll provide you with practical problem-solving techniques to face your fears head-on, step by step.

Understanding Fearlessness

Defining Fearlessness: We'll start by clarifying that fearlessness isn't about never experiencing fear but having the courage and skills to confront it effectively.

The Power of Courage: Explore how courage plays a significant role in problem-solving and fearlessness. Understand that courage can be developed and strengthened.

Practical Problem-Solving for Fearlessness

Fear Deconstruction: Apply problem-solving principles to deconstruct your fears. Break them down into manageable components and identify the specific aspects that trigger anxiety.

Risk Assessment: Use problem-solving techniques to assess the risks associated with confronting your fears. This systematic approach can provide a sense of control.

Step-by-Step Fear Confrontation

Gradual Exposure: Start by gradually exposing yourself to the source of your fear in a controlled manner. This stepwise approach helps desensitize you.

Problem-Solving Action Plans: Create problem-solving action plans for each fear you're confronting. Define the steps you'll take, potential challenges, and contingency plans.

Coping Strategies for Fear Confrontation

Stress Reduction Techniques: Apply problem-solving to identify stress reduction techniques that work for you. Managing stress can bolster your ability to confront fear.

Positive Visualization: Use problem-solving to develop positive mental images of yourself successfully facing your fears. Visualization can enhance your confidence.

Feedback and Adaptation

Feedback Loop: Establish a feedback loop for your fear-confrontation efforts. Regularly assess your progress and adjust your problem-solving action plans as needed.

Learning from Each Fear: Embrace each fear as an opportunity for growth. Apply problem-solving to extract insights and lessons from your fear-confrontation experiences.

Conclusion: Fearlessness as a Problem-Solving Skill

Fearlessness is not an innate trait but a skill that can be developed through problem-solving. By systematically deconstructing your fears, creating action plans, and confronting them step by step, you build the courage and resilience needed to face life's challenges fearlessly. As we continue in this chapter, we'll explore additional strategies for nurturing adaptability, fostering independence, and applying empowerment to overcome a wide range of obstacles.

Section 4: The Journey Ahead

Step 7: Embracing a Confident, Fearless Future

As we conclude this chapter, we'll reflect on the journey you've embarked on. By integrating problem-solving into your life, you're not only building self-confidence and conquering fear, but you're also fostering your mental well-being and personal growth.

In this chapter, we've shifted our focus from business to the realms of self-confidence and fear. Problem-solving is your ally on this journey, enabling you to build the self-confidence you need to confront your fears. As you master the art of problem-solving, you'll find yourself stepping boldly into the future, ready to embrace the challenges that come your way with unwavering confidence.

Section 1: The Connection Between Problem-Solving and Self-Confidence

Step 2: Problem-Solving as a Confidence Builder

Effective problem-solving isn't just about finding solutions; it's about believing in your ability to find those solutions. We'll explore how problem-solving can boost your self-confidence by demonstrating your competence and resourcefulness.

- Confidence in Your Abilities: As you successfully tackle problems and overcome obstacles using problem-solving techniques, you'll witness firsthand your own competence and capabilities. This newfound confidence in your abilities will extend beyond problem-solving and permeate other areas of your life.

- Resourcefulness: Problem-solving encourages you to think creatively and find innovative solutions. This resourcefulness not only helps you resolve issues but also reinforces your belief that you can adapt and thrive in different situations, further enhancing your self-confidence.

Section 2: Overcoming Fear with Problem-Solving

Step 3: Understanding Fear and Its Impact

Fear can be a formidable barrier to personal growth and mental well-being. In this step, we'll examine the various forms of fear and how they can hold you back from reaching your full potential.

• Fear of Failure: One of the most common fears is the fear of failure. It can paralyze you, preventing you from taking risks or pursuing your goals. Problem-solving equips you with the tools to assess and mitigate risks, making failure less daunting.

• Fear of the Unknown: The unknown can be a source of anxiety and fear. Problem-solving encourages you to break down the unknown into manageable pieces, making it less intimidating and more approachable.

Step 4: Problem-Solving as Fear Conqueror

Problem-solving is a structured approach to facing challenges, including your fears. We'll delve into how problem-solving techniques can help you confront and overcome fear by breaking it down into manageable components.

• Deconstructing Fear: Just as you dissect complex problems into smaller, solvable parts, you can break down your fears into manageable components. This allows you to address each aspect of your fear systematically, reducing its overwhelming impact.

• Building Courage: Problem-solving requires courage and determination to tackle difficult issues. As you apply problem-solving techniques to your fears, you'll gradually build your courage muscle, making it easier to confront fear in the future.

Section 3: Practical Problem-Solving for Confidence and Fearlessness

Step 5: Applying Problem-Solving to Self-Confidence Building

Building self-confidence is an ongoing journey. We'll explore practical problem-solving strategies that you can apply to boost your self-assurance and maintain it in your everyday life.

• Goal Setting: Utilize problem-solving techniques to set and achieve small, manageable goals. Each accomplishment reinforces your self-confidence and motivates you to take on more significant challenges.

• Positive Self-Talk: Problem-solving involves a rational, solution-focused mindset. Apply this mindset to challenge negative self-talk and replace it with self-affirming thoughts, further enhancing your self-confidence.

Step 6: Problem-Solving Your Way to Fearlessness (Continued)

Fearlessness doesn't mean the absence of fear but the ability to confront it courageously. In this step, we'll provide you with practical problem-solving techniques to face your fears head-on, step by step.

- Fear Exposure: Gradual exposure to your fears, combined with problem-solving strategies, can help you desensitize and eventually conquer them. This method, often used in cognitive-behavioral therapy, is a powerful tool in your journey to fearlessness.

- Visualization: Problem-solving involves planning and visualization. Apply these skills to mentally rehearse facing your fears successfully, boosting your confidence and readiness.

Section 4: The Journey Ahead

Step 7: Embracing a Confident, Fearless Future

As we conclude this chapter, we'll reflect on the journey you've embarked on. By integrating problem-solving into your life, you're not only building self-confidence and conquering fear, but you're also fostering your mental well-being and personal growth.

A Future Full of Possibilities

Empowerment Recap: Summarize the key takeaways from this chapter, emphasizing the empowerment you've gained through problem-solving.

Self-Confidence and Fearlessness: Reflect on how you've applied problem-solving techniques to build self-confidence and confront fear. Highlight specific achievements and milestones.

Mental Well-being: Recognize the connection between problem-solving, self-confidence, and mental well-being. Understand that your newfound skills contribute to your overall emotional health.

A Vision for the Future

Embracing Opportunities: Understand that, armed with problem-solving skills, self-confidence, and fear-conquering strategies, your future is full of possibilities. You're prepared to embrace opportunities with courage and determination.

Unwavering Confidence: Emphasize the importance of maintaining unwavering confidence in the face of challenges. You have the tools to tackle obstacles and setbacks with resilience.

Problem-Solving as a Lifelong Companion

A Lifelong Journey: Reiterate that problem-solving is not a one-time effort but a lifelong companion on your journey to personal growth and mental well-being.

Continuous Learning: Embrace the idea that you'll continue to refine your problem-solving skills, self-confidence, and fear-conquering strategies throughout your life.

Conclusion: The Empowered Future Awaits

As we conclude this chapter, remember that an empowered future awaits you. By integrating problem-solving into your life, you've embarked on a path to personal growth, mental well-being, and fearlessness. Armed with self-confidence and the ability to confront fear, you're ready to tackle any challenge that comes your way. The journey ahead is filled with opportunities, and with your newfound empowerment, you're poised to seize them with confidence, resilience, and a fearless spirit.

In this chapter, we've shifted our focus from business to the realms of self-confidence and fear. Problem-solving is your ally on this journey, enabling you to build the self-confidence you need to confront your fears. As you master the art of problem-solving, you'll find yourself stepping boldly into the future, ready to embrace the challenges that come your way with unwavering confidence.

"Believe in yourself and all that you are. Know that there is something inside you that is greater than any obstacle."

— Christian D. Larson

Chapter 7: Problem-Solving for Enhanced Mental Well-Being

In this chapter, we delve into the transformative power of problem-solving in the context of mental health. Problem-solving isn't just a practical tool; it's a mental wellness strategy that can empower you to navigate life's challenges and build resilience. We'll explore how problem-solving can contribute to your mental well-being and provide practical steps to harness its benefits.

Section 1: The Intersection of Problem-Solving and Mental Health

Step 1: Understanding the Mind-Body Connection

Let's start by acknowledging the profound link between your mental and physical well-being. Stress, anxiety, and depression often manifest physically, impacting your overall health. In this step, we'll explore the mind-body connection and how effective problem-solving can alleviate these symptoms.

The Mind-Body Connection

Holistic Wellness: Understand that your well-being encompasses both your mental and physical health. The mind and body are intricately linked, and changes in one can affect the other.

Physical Manifestations of Stress: Explore how stress, anxiety, and depression can manifest physically. These symptoms might include muscle tension, headaches, digestive issues, and more.

The Impact of Mental Health on Problem-Solving

Cognitive Function: Recognize that mental health issues can impair cognitive functions essential for problem-solving, such as concentration, memory, and decision-making.

Emotional Regulation: Understand that mental health challenges can disrupt emotional regulation, making it challenging to approach problems with a clear and rational mindset.

Problem-Solving as a Tool for Stress Management

Stress Reduction: Learn how effective problem-solving can alleviate stress by addressing its underlying causes. When you tackle problems systematically, stressors become more manageable.

Enhanced Coping Skills: Understand that problem-solving equips you with enhanced coping skills. You'll be better prepared to face and manage the challenges that contribute to stress.

Applying Problem-Solving to Mental Health

Identifying Stressors: Use problem-solving to identify and define the stressors in your life. You can do this, by pinpointing specific issues, and then, you can work toward solutions.

Creating Action Plans: Develop problem-solving action plans for addressing stressors. These plans outline steps to resolve or mitigate the issues contributing to stress.

Daily Practices for Mind-Body Wellness

Mindfulness and Relaxation: Incorporate mindfulness and relaxation techniques into your daily routine. Problem-solving can help you identify when and how to apply these practices effectively.

Physical Activity: Understand the role of physical activity in promoting mental health. Use problem-solving to create fitness plans that align with your goals and schedule.

Conclusion: A Balanced Approach to Mental Health

Recognize that mental health is an integral part of your overall well-being. By understanding the mind-body connection and applying problem-solving to address mental health challenges, you can achieve a more balanced and holistic approach to wellness. As we progress in this section, we'll explore additional strategies and exercises to promote mental health, foster resilience, and enhance problem-solving skills.

Step 2: Problem-Solving as a Stress Management Tool

Stress can take a toll on your mental health. However, effective problem-solving can be your shield against stress. We'll dive into how approaching life's challenges with a structured problem-solving mindset can help you manage and reduce stress levels.

The Impact of Stress on Mental Health

Stress as a Precursor to Mental Health Challenges: Understand that chronic stress can contribute to mental health issues like anxiety and depression. Recognize the importance of addressing stress proactively.

Physical and Emotional Toll: Explore how stress can manifest physically (e.g., headaches, muscle tension) and emotionally (e.g., irritability, mood swings).

Problem-Solving as a Stress Management Tool

Structured Approach to Challenges: Learn how a structured problem-solving approach helps you break down and address challenges systematically. This structured mindset can reduce the feeling of being overwhelmed.

Sense of Control: Understand that effective problem-solving can give you a sense of control over your circumstances. This sense of control is crucial for managing stress.

Applying Problem-Solving to Stress Management

Identifying Stressors: Use problem-solving techniques to identify the specific stressors in your life. List them systematically, so you have a clear understanding of what you're dealing with.

Creating Action Plans: Develop problem-solving action plans for each stressor. Define concrete steps to either resolve or mitigate the issues contributing to your stress.

Daily Stress Management Practices

Stress Journal: Maintain a stress journal where you document your daily stressors, your emotional responses, and your problem-solving efforts to address them.

Mindfulness and Relaxation: Incorporate mindfulness and relaxation techniques into your daily routine. Problem-solving can help you determine when and how to apply these practices effectively.

Feedback and Adaptation

Assess Progress: Regularly assess how your problem-solving efforts are impacting your stress levels. Are you experiencing reduced stress symptoms? Use this feedback to refine your strategies.

Adaptation: Understand that stress management is an ongoing process. Be open to adapting your problem-solving approaches as needed to effectively manage stressors.

Conclusion: Stress Management through Problem-Solving

Effective problem-solving is a potent tool for managing and reducing stress. By applying a structured problem-solving mindset to identify stressors, create action plans, and proactively address challenges, you empower yourself to take control of your mental well-being. As we continue in this section, we'll explore additional strategies and exercises to promote mental health, foster resilience, and enhance problem-solving skills, further enriching your stress management toolkit.

Section 2: Building Resilience through Problem-Solving

Step 3: Problem-Solving as Resilience Training

Resilience is your ability to bounce back from setbacks. In this step, we'll explore how problem-solving serves as resilience training. By tackling problems head-on, you can enhance your resilience and better weather life's storms.

Understanding Resilience

Defining Resilience: Begin by defining resilience as the ability to bounce back from adversity, setbacks, or challenges. It's a crucial life skill that contributes to mental well-being.

The Importance of Resilience: Emphasize why resilience is essential for navigating life's ups and downs. Resilient individuals can adapt and grow through adversity.

Problem-Solving as Resilience Training

Resilience Building: Explore how problem-solving inherently involves facing challenges and finding solutions. This process of confronting and overcoming obstacles is a form of resilience training.

Developing Adaptability: Understand that resilience and adaptability are closely linked. Problem-solving helps you develop the adaptability needed to thrive in changing circumstances.

Applying Problem-Solving to Resilience Building

Recognizing Challenges: Problem-solving begins by identifying challenges. Learn to recognize life's adversities as opportunities to enhance your resilience.

Tackling Setbacks: Apply problem-solving principles to setbacks. Develop action plans to address setbacks, bounce back, and move forward.

Daily Resilience Practices

Journaling: Maintain a resilience journal where you document your resilience-building efforts, challenges you've faced, and how problem-solving played a role in your ability to overcome them.

Self-Reflection: Regularly self-reflect on your resilience journey. Identify areas where you've grown stronger and how problem-solving has contributed to your resilience.

Feedback and Adaptation

Assess Resilience: Regularly assess your resilience levels. How have your problem-solving efforts impacted your ability to bounce back from setbacks?

Adaptation: Be open to adapting your problem-solving strategies as you encounter different challenges. Each experience is an opportunity to refine your resilience skills.

Conclusion: Problem-Solving as Resilience Training

Problem-solving isn't just about finding answers; it's a form of resilience training. By embracing challenges, developing adaptability, and systematically addressing setbacks, you're actively building your resilience. As you continue through this section, you'll further explore how problem-solving can be a powerful tool for fostering resilience, enhancing mental well-being, and promoting personal growth.

Step 4: Adapting to Change

Change is a constant in life, and adaptability is a key component of resilience. Effective problem solvers are inherently adaptable. We'll delve into how problem-solving skills can help you adjust to life's twists and turns, fostering mental well-being through change.

The Role of Adaptability in Resilience

Defining Adaptability: Begin by defining adaptability as the ability to adjust to new conditions and changes in your environment or circumstances.

The Connection to Resilience: Explore how adaptability and resilience are closely intertwined. Understand that adaptability is a crucial skill for bouncing back from adversity.

Problem-Solving Skills and Adaptability

Problem-Solving Mindset: Recognize that a problem-solving mindset encourages flexibility and open-mindedness. Problem solvers are more willing to adapt to changing situations.

Coping with Uncertainty: Understand how problem-solving can help you cope with uncertainty. By breaking down complex problems, you can approach unknown situations with more confidence.

Applying Problem-Solving to Adaptation

Recognizing Change: Use problem-solving skills to recognize changes in your life, whether they're major life transitions or daily adjustments.

Creating Flexible Plans: Develop problem-solving action plans that are adaptable. These plans should allow for adjustments as new information or challenges arise.

Daily Practices for Adaptability

Embracing Change: Cultivate a mindset that embraces change as an opportunity for growth. Reflect on how your problem-solving skills have helped you adapt to past changes.

Continuous Learning: Understand that adaptability is an ongoing process. Use problem-solving to identify areas where you can continue to enhance your adaptability skills.

Feedback and Adaptation

Self-Assessment: Regularly assess your adaptability levels. How have your problem-solving efforts contributed to your ability to adjust to change?

Flexibility in Problem-Solving: Be open to adapting your problem-solving approaches as you encounter new challenges. Flexibility in problem-solving translates to adaptability in life.

Conclusion: Problem-Solving and Adaptability

Adaptability is a cornerstone of resilience, and problem-solving skills can significantly enhance your adaptability. By embracing change, developing flexible problem-solving strategies, and recognizing the opportunities for growth that come with adaptation, you'll foster mental well-being and become better equipped to navigate life's ever-changing landscape. As we continue in this section, you'll explore more ways in which problem-solving can promote resilience, enhance mental health, and contribute to personal growth.

Section 3: Practical Problem-Solving for Mental Wellness

Step 5: Problem-Solving for Goal Achievement

Goals are essential for personal growth and mental well-being. Effective problem solvers excel in setting and achieving goals. We'll explore how problem-solving can bridge the gap between setting intentions and turning them into reality.

Understanding the Importance of Goals

Defining Goals: Begin by defining what goals are and why they are vital for personal growth and mental well-being. Goals give life purpose and direction.

The Role of Problem-Solving: Introduce the idea that effective problem solvers are more adept at setting, planning, and achieving their goals.

Problem-Solving for Goal Achievement

Setting SMART Goals: Explain the concept of SMART goals (Specific, Measurable, Achievable, Relevant, Time-bound) and how problem-solving can help in creating such goals.

Creating Action Plans: Emphasize that problem-solving extends to developing detailed action plans to achieve your goals. These plans involve identifying challenges and finding solutions.

Applying Problem-Solving to Goal Achievement

Goal Setting: Use problem-solving techniques to set clear and well-defined goals. Problem solvers excel in breaking down long-term objectives into manageable steps.

Creating Roadmaps: Develop problem-solving action plans that outline the specific steps required to achieve your goals. These plans serve as your roadmap to success.

Daily Practices for Goal Achievement

Goal Reflection: Reflect daily on your goals, the progress you've made, and any challenges you've encountered. Problem-solving can help you adapt your plans as needed.

Celebrate Milestones: Celebrate small victories along the way. Recognize how problem-solving has contributed to your progress.

Feedback and Adaptation

Goal Assessment: Regularly assess your progress toward your goals. How has your problem-solving approach impacted your ability to achieve them?

Adaptability in Goal Pursuit: Be open to adapting your problem-solving strategies when facing obstacles or changes in your goals. Problem-solving skills enhance your flexibility in achieving what matters to you.

Step 6: Problem-Solving and Emotional Regulation

Emotions often run high when facing life's challenges. Problem-solving encourages a rational approach, leading to better emotional regulation. In this step, we'll delve into how problem-solving can help you manage your emotions and maintain mental well-being.

Understanding Emotions and Problem-Solving

Emotional Responses to Challenges: Recognize that facing challenges often elicits strong emotional responses. Explore how emotions can either hinder or enhance problem-solving.

Rational Problem-Solving: Introduce the concept of using problem-solving to approach challenges with a rational and solution-oriented mindset. Problem solvers are less likely to be overwhelmed by emotions.

Problem-Solving for Emotional Regulation

Identifying Emotional Triggers: Use problem-solving to identify the specific challenges or situations that trigger intense emotions. By understanding the root causes, you can address them more effectively.

Developing Coping Strategies: Apply problem-solving to develop coping strategies that help you manage and regulate your emotions when facing stressors or setbacks.

Daily Practices for Emotional Regulation

Emotion Journal: Maintain a journal where you document your emotional responses to challenges and your problem-solving efforts to manage those emotions.

Mindfulness and Emotional Regulation: Explore how mindfulness practices can complement problem-solving in regulating emotions. Problem solvers can use mindfulness to stay present and composed.

Feedback and Adaptation

Emotional Progress: Regularly assess how your problem-solving efforts have impacted your emotional regulation. Are you better equipped to handle challenging emotions?

Flexible Emotional Responses: Be open to adapting your emotional responses to challenges as you refine your problem-solving skills. Problem solvers can approach emotional situations with greater flexibility.

Conclusion: Problem-Solving for Mental Wellness

Problem-solving is not just a tool for addressing external challenges; it's a valuable resource for setting and achieving goals and managing emotions effectively. By utilizing problem-solving to create clear goals, develop action plans, and regulate emotions, you'll enhance your mental well-being, foster resilience, and continue on the path of personal growth. As we move forward in this section, you'll explore additional problem-solving strategies and exercises to further enrich your mental wellness toolkit.

Section 4: Navigating Life's Challenges

Step 7: Conflict Resolution and Positive Relationships

Life challenges often involve conflicts with others. Effective problem solvers excel at resolving conflicts and building positive relationships. We'll discuss how these skills contribute to your mental well-being and overall happiness.

Understanding Conflict Resolution and Positive Relationships

Conflict in Life: Acknowledge that conflicts with others are a natural part of life. They can arise in personal, professional, and social settings.

The Role of Problem-Solving: Introduce the idea that problem-solving can be applied to conflict resolution, helping you address differences constructively.

Problem-Solving for Conflict Resolution

Conflict Identification: Use problem-solving to identify the root causes and issues contributing to conflicts. Problem solvers excel at distinguishing between surface-level disagreements and deeper concerns.

Negotiation and Compromise: Explore how problem-solving skills enable you to negotiate and find compromises that are acceptable to all parties involved in a conflict.

Building Positive Relationships

Communication: Emphasize the importance of effective communication in building positive relationships. Problem solvers are often adept communicators, which fosters understanding and empathy.

Problem-Solving in Relationships: Discuss how applying problem-solving principles in personal relationships can lead to healthier interactions and resolutions.

Daily Practices for Conflict Resolution and Relationship Building

Conflict Journal: Maintain a journal where you document conflicts you encounter and the problem-solving strategies you use to resolve them.

Active Listening: Practice active listening, a skill often enhanced by problem solvers, to understand others' perspectives in conflicts.

Feedback and Adaptation

Conflict Resolution Progress: Regularly assess your progress in resolving conflicts using problem-solving. Have your relationships improved as a result?

Building Better Relationships: Continuously work on improving your relationships by applying problem-solving and seeking feedback from others.

Step 8: A Lifelong Journey of Learning

Problem-solving is a continuous learning process. Each problem you encounter provides an opportunity to gain new insights and skills. We'll explore how this lifelong learning contributes to personal growth and mental well-being.

Embracing Continuous Learning

Problem-Solving as Learning: Understand that every problem you solve is an opportunity to learn and grow. Problem solvers approach challenges with curiosity and a desire for improvement.

Acquiring New Skills: Explore how problem-solving naturally leads to the acquisition of various skills, from analytical thinking to effective communication.

Problem-Solving for Personal Growth

Setting Challenges: Use problem-solving to set personal challenges that push your boundaries and encourage growth.

Learning from Mistakes: Embrace mistakes and failures as opportunities for learning and refinement of problem-solving strategies.

Daily Practices for Lifelong Learning

Challenge Yourself: Regularly seek out challenges that require problem-solving. These can be related to your personal life, career, or hobbies.

Reflection and Improvement: After solving a problem, take time to reflect on the process. What did you learn, and how can you apply this knowledge in the future?

Feedback and Adaptation

Measuring Personal Growth: Continuously assess your personal growth and development. How have your problem-solving experiences contributed to your growth?

Adapting to New Challenges: Be open to adapting your problem-solving approaches as you encounter new and more complex challenges. Problem solvers thrive on continuous improvement.

Conclusion: Lifelong Learning through Problem-Solving

Problem-solving is not just a tool for addressing immediate challenges; it's a pathway to continuous learning and personal growth. By applying problem-solving to conflict resolution, building positive relationships, and seeking challenges that push your boundaries, you'll embark on a lifelong journey of learning and self-improvement. This journey contributes significantly to your mental well-being and overall happiness. As we conclude this section, you'll have a comprehensive toolkit for using problem-solving to enhance various aspects of your life.

In this chapter, we've shifted the focus from business to your mental well-being. By mastering problem-solving skills, you can not only overcome obstacles but also enhance your mental health, reduce stress, and develop resilience. Embrace problem-solving as a powerful tool on your journey toward improved mental well-being and personal growth.

"The journey of a thousand miles begins with one step." — Lao Tzu

Chapter 8: Building Resilience and Adaptation in the Face of Change

Section 1: Understanding Resilience

Resilience is the ability to bounce back from adversity and adapt positively to change. It's a crucial skill for navigating life's ups and downs effectively.

Step 1: Embrace Change as a Constant

Change is a fundamental part of life. Embracing it as a constant rather than an exception is the first step in building resilience.

To embrace change effectively:

- Mindset Shift: Adopt a growth mindset that welcomes change as an opportunity for learning and growth.

- Acceptance: Accept that not all changes are within your control. Focus on what you can influence and let go of what you cannot.

- Flexibility: Cultivate flexibility in your thinking and actions. Being adaptable is key to resilience.

Step 2: Prioritizing Mental Health

Your mental health is the foundation of resilience. Taking care of your well-being equips you to face challenges with greater strength.

To prioritize mental health effectively:

• Self-Care: Establish self-care routines that nurture your mental and emotional well-being. This can include meditation, exercise, journaling, and hobbies.

• Seek Support: Don't hesitate to seek support from friends, family, or mental health professionals when needed. Talking about your feelings can be immensely beneficial.

• Mindfulness: Practice mindfulness to stay present and reduce stress. Mindfulness techniques can help you stay grounded during times of change.

Section 2: Building Resilience

Building resilience is an ongoing process. It involves developing skills and strategies to navigate change and adversity effectively.

Step 3: Problem-Solving Skills

Effective problem-solving skills are a cornerstone of resilience. They enable you to approach challenges with a clear plan of action.

To enhance problem-solving skills effectively:

- Define the Problem: Clearly define the problem or challenge you're facing. Break it down into manageable components.

- Generate Solutions: Brainstorm potential solutions. Consider multiple approaches before settling on a plan.

- Take Action: Implement your chosen solution and monitor its progress. Be open to adjustments along the way.

Step 4: Building a Support System

A strong support system provides emotional, practical, and social support during challenging times.

To build a support system effectively:

- Identify Supportive People: Recognize the people in your life who provide support and seek out their assistance when needed.

- Network Building: Expand your social network by joining groups or communities that share your interests or values.

- Reciprocity: Offer support to others in your network. Building a supportive community is a two-way street.

Step 5: Emotional Regulation*

Emotional regulation is the ability to manage your emotions in a healthy and constructive manner.

To regulate your emotions effectively:

- Awareness: Develop self-awareness by recognizing your emotional responses to different situations.

- Emotion Expression: Express your emotions in a healthy way, whether through journaling, talking with a trusted friend, or engaging in creative outlets.

- Stress Reduction: Learn stress reduction techniques such as deep breathing exercises and progressive muscle relaxation.

Section 3: Adaptation and Coping Skills

Adaptation is about adjusting to new circumstances and developing coping skills that enable you to thrive despite challenges.

Step 6: Cognitive Flexibility

Cognitive flexibility is the ability to adapt your thinking and problem-solving approach when faced with new information or changing circumstances.

To enhance cognitive flexibility effectively:

• Question Assumptions: Challenge your assumptions and be open to considering alternative perspectives.

• Learn Continuously: Seek out new information and perspectives. Learning keeps your mind flexible.

• Practice Mental Exercises: Engage in puzzles, brain teasers, or games that require you to think in different ways.

Step 7: Resilience-Building Mindset

A resilience-building mindset involves a positive outlook on challenges and a belief in your ability to overcome them.

To cultivate a resilience-building mindset effectively:

• Positive Self-Talk: Challenge negative self-talk and replace it with affirmations of your capabilities.

• Visualize Success: Visualize yourself successfully navigating challenges. This can boost your confidence.

• Learn from Setbacks: View setbacks as opportunities for growth and learning rather than as failures.

This section has introduced the importance of resilience, mental health, and adaptation skills in facing life's challenges. In the next section, we'll explore strategies for thriving in a changing world and the importance of flexibility in today's dynamic environment.

Section 4: Thriving in a Changing World

In today's fast-paced and ever-changing world, the ability to thrive amidst constant shifts and uncertainty is a valuable skill. This section explores strategies to not only survive but to thrive in a dynamic environment.

Step 8: Continuous Learning

Continuous learning is the cornerstone of thriving in a changing world. It involves actively seeking knowledge and skills to adapt to new challenges.

To engage in continuous learning effectively:

•   Stay Curious: Cultivate a curious mindset. Approach new information and experiences with a thirst for knowledge.

•   Set Learning Goals: Define clear learning goals for yourself. Whether it's acquiring a new skill or understanding a complex topic, goals provide direction.

•   Diverse Sources: Explore diverse sources of learning, including books, courses, workshops, and online resources.

Step 9: Agility and Flexibility

Agility and flexibility are essential for thriving in a rapidly changing environment. Being able to pivot and adapt to new circumstances is a valuable skill.

To enhance agility and flexibility effectively:

•   Embrace Change: Rather than resisting change, embrace it. See it as an opportunity to grow and evolve.

•   Scenario Planning: Consider different scenarios and prepare contingency plans. This helps you respond swiftly to unexpected changes.

•   Feedback-Driven Adaptation: Regularly gather feedback and adjust your strategies accordingly. Be open to making quick changes based on new information.

Step 10: Building Resilient Networks

Your professional and personal networks play a crucial role in your ability to thrive. Building resilient networks involves fostering connections that can support you in times of change.

To build resilient networks effectively:

- Networking Skills: Develop your networking skills, such as active listening, relationship-building, and maintaining connections.

- Diverse Connections: Cultivate a diverse network that includes individuals from various backgrounds, industries, and perspectives.

- Reciprocity: Offer support and assistance to your network. Being a valuable resource to others strengthens your network's resilience.

Section 5: Embracing Creativity

Creativity is a powerful tool for thriving in a changing world. It enables you to generate innovative solutions and adapt to new challenges.

Step 11: Nurturing Creativity

To nurture creativity effectively:

- Creativity Practices: Engage in creative practices such as brainstorming, mind mapping, or artistic endeavors to keep your creative juices flowing.

• Cross-Disciplinary Learning: Explore topics and disciplines outside your usual areas of interest. This cross-pollination of ideas can spark creativity.

• Downtime: Allow yourself periods of downtime for relaxation and reflection. Often, creativity emerges during moments of relaxation.

Step 12: Innovation Mindset

Cultivating an innovation mindset involves being open to new ideas, approaches, and technologies.

To develop an innovation mindset effectively:

• Embrace Change: As mentioned earlier, embrace change as an opportunity for innovation rather than a threat.

• Experimentation: Be willing to experiment with new approaches and technologies. Not every experiment needs to lead to a breakthrough, but each one can teach you something valuable.

• Feedback-Driven Improvement: Seek feedback on your innovative ideas and adapt based on the insights you gather.

This section has explored strategies for thriving in a changing world, including continuous learning, agility, building resilient networks, and embracing creativity. In the next section, we'll conclude this chapter and provide a preview of Chapter 9, which explores the role of leadership in effective problem solving.

Section 6: Conclusion and Transition to Chapter 9

In this concluding section of Chapter 8, we'll summarize the key takeaways on building resilience and thriving in a changing world. Additionally, we'll provide a glimpse of what to expect in Chapter 9, where we'll explore the role of leadership in effective problem solving.

Step 13: Summary of Key Takeaways

Throughout this chapter, we've explored the vital skills and strategies for building resilience and thriving in an ever-changing environment. Here are the key takeaways to remember:

• Embrace Change: Embrace change as a constant in life and view it as an opportunity for growth.

- Prioritize Mental Health: Your mental and emotional well-being is the foundation of resilience. Practice self-care and seek support when needed.

- Problem-Solving Skills: Effective problem-solving skills are a cornerstone of resilience. Develop the ability to define problems, generate solutions, and take action.

- Cognitive Flexibility: Cultivate cognitive flexibility to adapt your thinking and problem-solving approach as circumstances change.

- Continuous Learning: Lifelong learning is essential for thriving in a dynamic world. Stay curious and set clear learning goals.

- Creativity and Innovation: Nurture your creativity and develop an innovation mindset to generate novel solutions.

"Believe you can
and you're halfway
there."

— Theodore Roosevelt

Chapter 9: Evaluating Self-Efforts, Learning from Results, and Cultivating Mental Health and Self-Sufficiency

Section 1: Assessing Self-Efforts and Results

This section explores the importance of assessing your self-efforts and the results of your problem-solving journey. It provides guidance on how to effectively evaluate your progress.

Step 1: Self-Effort Assessment

Self-effort assessment involves reflecting on the actions, strategies, and dedication you've put into your problem-solving endeavors.

To assess self-efforts effectively:

• Reflection: Take time to reflect on the effort you've invested. Consider the dedication, time, and resources you've committed.

• Goal Alignment: Evaluate whether your self-efforts aligned with your goals and priorities. Were they focused on the right areas?

• Growth and Learning: Consider how your self-efforts contributed to personal growth and learning. Did you acquire new skills or knowledge along the way?

Step 2: Results Evaluation

Evaluating the results of your problem-solving efforts is crucial for understanding what worked, what didn't, and what you can improve.

To evaluate results effectively:

• Goal Achievement: Assess whether you achieved your desired outcomes. Did you meet your goals, and if not, what were the reasons?

• Data Analysis: Utilize data and evidence to analyze the impact of your efforts. Data-driven insights provide valuable information.

• Feedback Collection: Gather feedback from stakeholders and those affected by your solutions. Their perspectives can offer valuable insights.

Section 2: Learning from the Process

Learning from the problem-solving process is a continuous journey. It involves identifying lessons, adjusting strategies, and evolving as a problem solver.

Step 3: Identifying Lessons

Identifying lessons involves recognizing what you've learned from both your successes and setbacks.

To identify lessons effectively:

• Post-Mortem Analysis: Conduct post-mortem analyses after completing projects or solving problems. What went well? What could have been improved?

• Success and Failure: Don't only focus on successes. Analyze your failures and setbacks. What can you learn from them?

• Peer Feedback: Seek feedback from peers or mentors who can offer valuable perspectives on your problem-solving journey.

Step 4: Adapting Strategies

Adapting your problem-solving strategies based on your learnings is crucial for continuous improvement.

To adapt strategies effectively:

• Iterative Approach: Embrace an iterative approach to problem solving. Be willing to make adjustments as you gain new insights.

• Test and Refine: Experiment with different approaches and refine your strategies based on the results.

• Flexibility: Cultivate flexibility in your problem-solving toolkit. What worked in one situation may not work in another.

Section 3: Mental Health Improvement and Self-Sufficiency

This section explores how the problem-solving process can positively influence mental health and contribute to self-sufficiency.

Step 5: Mental Health Benefits

Engaging in problem solving can have profound effects on mental health. It provides a sense of purpose, accomplishment, and empowerment.

To experience mental health benefits effectively:

- Stress Reduction: Problem solving can serve as a healthy outlet for stress. Focusing on solutions can alleviate anxiety.

- Sense of Control: Problem solvers often feel a greater sense of control over their lives, which can boost mental well-being.

- Confidence Building: Successfully navigating challenges can enhance self-confidence and resilience.

Step 6: Cultivating Self-Sufficiency

Self-sufficiency is the ability to rely on one's own resources and capabilities. Effective problem solving contributes to this self-reliance.

To cultivate self-sufficiency effectively:

- Skill Development: Problem solving hones various skills, from critical thinking to decision-making. These skills increase self-sufficiency.

- Resourcefulness: Problem solvers learn to be resourceful and creative, finding solutions even with limited resources.

- Empowerment: Self-sufficiency empowers individuals to take charge of their lives and navigate challenges independently.

This section has highlighted the importance of evaluating self-efforts, learning from results, and how the problem-solving process can influence mental health and self-sufficiency. In the next section, we'll explore how to apply the insights gained from this evaluation process effectively.

Section 4: Applying Your Learnings

This section focuses on how to apply the insights gained from evaluating your self-efforts, results, and the lessons learned throughout your problem-solving journey.

Step 7: Integration of Insights

Integrating your insights into your daily life and future problem-solving endeavors is key to personal growth and continuous improvement.

To integrate insights effectively:

• Actionable Takeaways: Identify actionable takeaways from your self-efforts assessment, results evaluation, and lessons learned.

- Goal Alignment: Align your future goals and problem-solving strategies with these insights. Ensure that you apply what you've learned.

- Regular Reflection: Make reflection a regular practice. Periodically revisit your insights to stay on course and make necessary adjustments.

Step 8: Share and Teach

Sharing your problem-solving experiences and knowledge with others can be both personally fulfilling and beneficial to your community.

To share and teach effectively:

- Mentorship: Consider mentoring others in problem solving, especially if you've gained expertise in a specific area.

- Workshops and Presentations: Host workshops or presentations to share your insights and lessons with a broader audience.

- Writing and Documentation: Document your problem-solving journey in writing. This could take the form of articles, blogs, or even a book.

Section 5: Personal Growth and Transformation

The problem-solving journey has the potential to catalyze personal growth and transformation. This section explores the transformative power of effective problem solving.

Step 9: Embracing Change

Embracing change is a core aspect of personal growth and transformation. As you apply your learnings, be open to evolving and adapting.

To embrace change effectively:

• Mindset Shift: Maintain a growth mindset that welcomes change as an opportunity for personal development.

• Continuous Learning: Continue seeking new knowledge and skills, even as you grow. Learning is a lifelong journey.

• Self-Reflection: Regularly self-reflect to assess your personal growth and areas where further development is needed.

Step 10: Cultivating Resilience

The resilience built through effective problem solving contributes significantly to personal growth and transformation.

To cultivate resilience effectively:

- Adaptive Thinking: Apply adaptive thinking to all aspects of your life. Be flexible and open to new perspectives.

- Seek Support: Lean on your support network during times of challenge or change. Don't hesitate to ask for help when needed.

- Celebrate Progress: Acknowledge and celebrate your growth and resilience. Recognize your accomplishments along the way.

Section 6: Conclusion

In this final section of Chapter 9, we'll summarize the key takeaways from the chapter and provide a transition to Chapter 10, where we'll explore the broader impact of effective problem solving on society and the world.

Step 11: Summary of Key Takeaways

Throughout this chapter, we've delved into the process of evaluating self-efforts, learning from results, and how effective problem solving can lead to mental health improvement and self-sufficiency. Here are the key takeaways to remember:

- Continuous Evaluation: Regularly assess your self-efforts, evaluate results, and learn from the process.

- Integration and Application: Apply the insights gained from evaluation to your future problem-solving endeavors and daily life.

- Sharing and Teaching: Consider sharing your problem-solving experiences and knowledge with others through mentoring, workshops, or writing.

- Personal Growth and Transformation: Effective problem solving has the potential to catalyze personal growth, resilience, and transformation.

Step 12: Looking Ahead to Chapter 10

As you conclude this chapter, reflect on how your problem-solving journey has contributed to your personal development. In Chapter 10, we'll explore the broader societal and global impact of effective problem solving.

Chapter 10: Problem Solving for a Better World

In Chapter 10, we'll dive into the significant role of problem solving in creating positive change on a larger scale. We'll explore:

- The importance of collective problem solving for addressing global challenges.

- Case studies and examples of how effective problem solving has transformed communities and societies.

- The ethical responsibilities that come with solving complex societal issues.

- How individuals and organizations can contribute to a better world through problem solving.

Stay tuned for a discussion on how effective problem solving can shape a brighter future for our world.

Chapter 10: Empowering Change Agents

Section 1: The Power of Collective Problem Solving

This section dives into the profound impact collective problem solving can have on mental health and personal growth, as individuals unite to address shared challenges.

Step 1: Understanding Collective Problem Solving

Collective problem solving transcends individual efforts by fostering collaboration among diverse individuals, creating a stronger sense of purpose and accomplishment.

To grasp collective problem solving effectively:

Identify Common Goals: Recognize shared objectives that unite individuals with diverse perspectives, reinforcing a collective sense of purpose.

Collaborative Mindset: Cultivate a mindset that values collaboration, appreciating the wealth of knowledge and experiences that different individuals bring to the table.

Responsibility and Impact: Understand that engaging in collective problem solving carries a profound responsibility for shaping a more positive and harmonious society.

Sample Scenario:

Imagine you are part of a support group focused on mental health and well-being. Together, you work to raise awareness, share resources, and support one another in your individual journeys toward better mental health. Your collective effort not only strengthens your own resilience but also helps countless others on their path to healing and growth.

Section 2: Case Studies and Examples

In this section, we'll explore real-world cases and examples that showcase the transformative potential of collective problem solving in the context of mental health and personal development.

Step 2: Case Study: Community Mental Health Initiative

Delve into a case study where a community came together to establish a comprehensive mental health initiative. Analyze the collaborative efforts, the impact on individual well-being, and the creation of a supportive network.

Step 3: Example: Online Peer Support Communities

Explore an example of online peer support communities that leverage collective problem solving to provide individuals with a platform for sharing experiences, coping strategies, and emotional support. Highlight the power of empathy and shared experiences in nurturing mental well-being.

Section 3: Ethical Responsibilities

Effective collective problem solving comes with ethical responsibilities. This section delves into the ethical considerations integral to addressing mental health and personal development as a group.

Step 4: Ethical Decision-Making in Collective Problem Solving

Ethical decision-making in collective problem solving encompasses respecting diverse perspectives, fostering inclusivity, and addressing ethical dilemmas.

To engage in ethical decision-making effectively:

Values Alignment: Ensure that the collective's values align with ethical principles, including empathy, respect, and a commitment to mental well-being.

Inclusivity: Promote inclusivity by welcoming diverse voices and experiences in decision-making processes. Acknowledge and honor individual differences.

Transparency and Accountability: Uphold transparency in actions and decisions, and hold the collective accountable for adhering to ethical commitments.

Sample Scenario:

Imagine you are part of a mental health advocacy group striving to destigmatize mental health issues in your community. Ethical dilemmas arise when deciding how to represent personal stories and experiences while respecting privacy. Ethical decision-making involves collaborating with mental health professionals, storytellers, and ethicists to strike a balance between raising awareness and protecting individuals' well-being.

Section 4: Contributions to Mental Health and Personal Growth

This section explores how collective problem solving can contribute to better mental health and personal growth, fostering a sense of belonging and purpose.

Step 5: Personal and Group Commitments

Both individuals and collectives can make commitments to address mental health challenges and support personal growth effectively.

To make commitments effectively:

Identify Areas of Impact: Identify the areas where you, as an individual or group, can make the most significant impact in supporting mental health and personal development.

Action Plans: Develop action plans that outline specific steps, objectives, and timelines for addressing mental health and personal growth.

Measurable Outcomes: Define measurable outcomes to track progress and assess the collective's positive influence on individual well-being.

Sample Guidance:

As an individual, you may commit to facilitating regular mindfulness sessions in your community to promote mental well-being. Your collective, on the other hand, may pledge to collaborate with local schools to implement mental health education programs, ensuring that the next generation grows up with the tools to support their own mental health.

This section has explored the potential of collective problem solving in enhancing mental health and personal growth. In the next section, we'll discuss how to empower individuals to become change agents within their communities and advocates for mental health and personal development on a broader scale.

Section 5: Becoming Change Agents

This section focuses on empowering individuals to become effective change agents in their communities, using collective problem solving as a means to nurture mental health and personal growth.

Step 6: Embracing the Change Agent Role

Becoming a change agent entails actively working toward the betterment of mental health and personal growth for oneself and others. It involves taking initiative, setting examples, and inspiring collective efforts.

To become a change agent effectively:

Identify Your Passion: Discover the areas within mental health and personal growth that ignite your passion and dedication. It's through your genuine care that you can drive meaningful change.

Lead by Example: Demonstrate the positive changes you wish to see in the world through your actions, decisions, and commitment.

Mobilize Resources: Connect with like-minded individuals, organizations, and resources to amplify your impact and collectively address mental health and personal development challenges.

Sample Guidance:

Imagine you have a deep passion for promoting self-compassion as a crucial component of mental well-being. You can become a change agent by organizing workshops, starting online support groups, and collaborating with mental health professionals to advocate for the inclusion of self-compassion practices in therapy.

Section 6: Navigating Challenges

Effecting change often comes with challenges and obstacles. This section explores how to navigate these challenges effectively, considering the unique context of mental health and personal growth.

Step 7: Overcoming Resistance

Resistance to change, especially in the realm of mental health and personal development, is common. Change agents must learn to navigate resistance sensitively.

To overcome resistance effectively:

Communication: Clearly communicate the benefits and reasons behind proposed changes in the context of mental well-being and personal growth.

Active Listening: Listen to concerns and objections from stakeholders, acknowledging their fears and providing evidence of the positive outcomes.

Compromise: Be open to compromise and finding common ground. Sometimes, gradual change is more acceptable than abrupt shifts in mental health approaches.

Step 8: Building Resilience as a Change Agent

Building resilience is vital for change agents, particularly in the sphere of mental health and personal development, where setbacks and opposition can be emotionally taxing.

To build resilience effectively:

Self-Care: Prioritize self-care to maintain mental and emotional well-being as you navigate the challenges of promoting mental health and personal growth.

Support Network: Lean on your support network for encouragement, advice, and a sense of community as you advocate for positive change.

Learning from Setbacks: View setbacks as opportunities for learning, growth, and refinement of your approach in the realm of mental well-being and personal development.

Section 7: Measuring Impact and Celebrating Success

This section underscores the importance of measuring the impact of change efforts and celebrating milestones in the context of mental health and personal growth.

Step 9: Impact Measurement

Measuring impact entails assessing the tangible outcomes and improvements in mental health and personal growth resulting from collective problem solving.

To measure impact effectively:

Data Collection: Gather relevant data and evidence to assess the effects of your initiatives, focusing on mental well-being and personal development indicators.

Defining Indicators: Define clear indicators and metrics that can track progress and improvements in mental health and personal growth.

Regular Assessment: Continuously assess the effectiveness of your efforts and make adjustments as needed to optimize outcomes related to mental well-being and personal development.

Sample Guidance:

Suppose you've been involved in a community-based mental health program aimed at reducing the stigma associated with seeking therapy. You can measure impact by tracking the number of individuals seeking therapy, monitoring changes in community attitudes toward mental health, and evaluating the program's influence on personal development and resilience.

Section 8: Conclusion and Call to Action

In this final section of Chapter 10, we'll recap the key takeaways and issue a call to action for readers to embrace their roles as change agents and advocates for mental health and personal development through collective problem solving.

Step 10: Summary of Key Takeaways

Throughout this chapter, we've explored the potential of collective problem solving in enhancing mental health and personal growth, addressed ethical considerations, discussed the contributions of individuals and collectives, empowered change agents, navigated challenges, measured impact, and celebrated success. Here are the key takeaways:

- Collective Effort: Collective problem solving can significantly impact mental health and personal growth by fostering a sense of community and purpose.

- Ethical Considerations: Ethical decision-making and inclusivity are crucial when addressing mental well-being and personal development collectively.

- Commitments: Individuals and groups can commit to initiatives that support mental health and personal growth, making a meaningful difference.

- Change Agent Role: Embracing the role of a change agent involves passion, leadership, and resource mobilization.

- Resilience and Impact: Change agents must navigate challenges, measure impact, and celebrate successes, particularly in the context of mental health and personal growth.

Step 11: Call to Action

As you conclude this chapter, consider the pivotal role you can play in fostering mental health, personal growth, and positive societal change. Embrace your potential as a change agent and collective problem solver in the realm of mental well-being and personal development. Whether advocating for mental health support, promoting self-compassion, or encouraging emotional well-being, your efforts can bring about transformative change.

With the completion of this chapter, we've covered the significance of collective problem solving in the context of mental health and personal growth. If you have any additional sections, themes, or topics you'd like to explore or specific requests for the book's conclusion or any other aspects, please feel free to share, and I'll be glad to assist further.

Chapter 11: The Journey Ahead - Sustaining Growth and Impact

Section 1: Sustaining Personal Growth

This section delves into strategies for sustaining the personal growth and development achieved through effective problem-solving skills.

Step 1: Lett's start for Reflecting on Your Journey

Reflection is a key element in sustaining personal growth. Take time to reflect on your problem-solving journey and its impact on your life.

To reflect effectively:

• Journaling: Maintain a journal to document your experiences, challenges, and lessons learned.

• Mentorship: Seek guidance and mentorship from experienced individuals who can help you navigate your continued growth.

• Gratitude: Express gratitude for the opportunities and support you've received along the way.

Step 2: Set New Goals

Continuous growth involves setting new goals and challenges. Define clear and meaningful goals that align with your evolving aspirations.

To set new goals effectively:

• SMART Goals: Use the SMART (Specific, Measurable, Achievable, Relevant, Time-bound) framework to structure your goals.

The SMART framework is a highly effective tool for goal setting and problem-solving, especially in the context of personal development and mental well-being. Let's dive deeper into each element of SMART goals:

1. Specific: When setting a goal, it's crucial to be as specific as possible about what you want to achieve. Vague goals can be challenging to work towards because you may not have a clear understanding of what success looks like. Being specific means defining the who, what, where, when, and why of your goal.

• Example: Instead of a vague goal like "improve my mental health," a specific goal would be "practice mindfulness meditation for 20 minutes every morning before work to reduce anxiety and stress."

2. Measurable: Measuring your progress is essential for tracking your success and staying motivated. Measurable goals allow you to quantify

your achievements, making it easier to determine if you're on the right track.

• Example: In the goal of practicing mindfulness meditation, the measurable aspect is the daily 20-minute meditation session. You can track your progress by checking off each completed session on a calendar or using a meditation app.

3. Achievable: Your goals should be realistic and attainable. Setting overly ambitious or unattainable goals can lead to frustration and demotivation. Consider your current resources, capabilities, and constraints when defining your goals.

• Example: If you've never meditated before, it might be unrealistic to aim for an hour-long meditation session each day. Starting with 20 minutes is more achievable and allows you to build your practice gradually.

4. Relevant: Ensure that your goals are relevant to your overall well-being and personal growth. They should align with your values, interests, and long-term objectives. Irrelevant goals can distract you from what truly matters.

• Example: If your main goal is to reduce stress and anxiety, a relevant goal like mindfulness meditation directly addresses that objective. On the other hand, setting a goal to learn a new language, while valuable, might not directly contribute to your immediate mental well-being.

5. Time-bound: Setting a timeframe for your goals creates a sense of urgency and helps prevent procrastination. It also allows you to break your goal down into smaller, manageable steps with specific deadlines.

• Example: Adding a time-bound element to your meditation goal could look like this: "Practice mindfulness meditation for 20 minutes every morning for the next 30 days." This timeframe provides structure and accountability.

Using the SMART framework for your goals in the context of personal development and mental well-being ensures that your objectives are well-defined, actionable, and aligned with your overall journey. It helps you stay focused, measure your progress, and ultimately achieve a greater sense of accomplishment and well-being.

• Stretch Goals: Incorporate stretch goals that push you beyond your comfort zone while remaining realistic.

Incorporating stretch goals into your personal development and mental well-being journey can be a powerful way to foster growth and resilience. Stretch goals are ambitious objectives that challenge you to go beyond your current abilities and comfort zone while remaining within the realm of achievability. Here's an in-depth look at the concept of stretch goals:

1. Pushing Beyond Comfort Zones: Stretch goals are designed to push you out of your comfort zone. They encourage you to explore new territories, take on challenges you might have otherwise avoided, and embrace discomfort as a catalyst for growth.

• Example: If you're working on building self-confidence, a stretch goal could involve speaking in public, even if you have a fear of public speaking. This might be uncomfortable initially, but it can lead to significant personal growth.

2. Expanding Your Limits: Stretch goals help you expand your perceived limits of what you can achieve. By setting goals that seem just beyond your current capabilities, you create opportunities for self-discovery and development.

• Example: If you're aiming to manage anxiety and stress, a stretch goal might be to participate in a stress-inducing but manageable situation, such as a challenging work presentation. Successfully navigating this experience can boost your confidence and resilience.

3. Learning and Adaptation: Pursuing stretch goals often requires learning new skills or acquiring additional knowledge. This learning

process can be intellectually stimulating and contribute to your personal growth.

• Example: If you're interested in improving your mental well-being through mindfulness, a stretch goal could involve attending a meditation retreat where you can deepen your practice and gain new insights into your mind.

4. Building Resilience: Stretch goals are inherently challenging, and they may involve setbacks and failures along the way. However, these setbacks provide valuable opportunities to develop resilience and adaptability, which are essential for mental well-being.

• Example: If you're setting a stretch goal to overcome a specific fear, such as flying, you might face moments of anxiety during the process. Learning to manage and bounce back from these moments can strengthen your resilience.

5. Maintaining Realism: While stretch goals are meant to challenge you, they should still be grounded in reality. It's essential to strike a balance between ambition and feasibility to prevent setting yourself up for unattainable objectives that could lead to frustration.

• Example: If you're working on improving your physical fitness, a stretch goal might be to complete a challenging marathon. However, ensure that you set this goal with consideration of your current fitness level and allow ample time for training and preparation.

6. Celebrating Progress: Celebrate your achievements, both small and large, as you work toward stretch goals. Recognizing your progress along the way can boost your motivation and provide a sense of accomplishment.

- Example: If your stretch goal involves weight loss, celebrate reaching incremental milestones, such as losing a certain number of pounds or fitting into a particular clothing size. Acknowledging these achievements can keep you motivated.

Incorporating stretch goals into your personal development and mental well-being journey encourages you to embrace challenges, expand your horizons, and develop resilience. When approached with a realistic yet ambitious mindset, stretch goals can be a catalyst for profound personal growth and a more fulfilling life.

- Long-Term Vision: Consider your long-term vision for personal and professional development.

Developing a long-term vision for personal and professional development is a crucial aspect of goal-setting and problem-solving in the context of mental well-being and self-improvement. Here's an in-depth exploration of the concept of a long-term vision:

1. Clarity of Purpose: Establishing a long-term vision provides you with clarity of purpose. It helps you define what you ultimately want to achieve in various aspects of your life, including personal growth, career, relationships, and mental well-being.

- Example: If your long-term vision is to have a fulfilling career in a field that aligns with your passions and values, you'll have a clear direction for your professional development.

2. Goal Alignment: Your long-term vision serves as a guiding compass for setting short-term and intermediate goals. It ensures that your goals are aligned with your overarching aspirations and values.

- Example: If your long-term vision involves maintaining optimal mental well-being, your short-term and intermediate goals might include daily mindfulness practice, stress management techniques, and seeking therapy when needed.

3. Motivation and Persistence: A long-term vision provides a source of motivation and inspiration. It helps you stay committed to your goals, even when faced with challenges or setbacks.

- Example: If your long-term vision is to build a strong support network of friends and loved ones for improved mental well-being, you'll be motivated to invest time and effort in nurturing those relationships, even during busy or challenging periods.

4. Planning and Strategy: Developing a long-term vision necessitates strategic planning. It encourages you to map out the steps and milestones required to reach your desired destination.

• Example: If your long-term vision involves achieving a high level of physical fitness, you'll need to create a comprehensive fitness plan that includes regular exercise, a balanced diet, and restorative practices.

5. Adaptability and Flexibility: A well-defined long-term vision also allows for adaptability. Life is dynamic, and circumstances may change. Your long-term vision can serve as a flexible framework that accommodates adjustments and pivots as needed.

• Example: If your long-term vision initially included a specific career path but you discover a new passion along the way, you can adapt your vision to incorporate this newfound interest into your overall development plan.

6. Holistic Well-Being: Your long-term vision should encompass various facets of well-being, including mental, emotional, physical, and social aspects. It encourages you to consider the interplay between these dimensions and prioritize a holistic approach to self-improvement.

• Example: If your long-term vision focuses on holistic well-being, you'll work on not only managing stress and anxiety but also nurturing positive relationships, maintaining physical health, and pursuing activities that bring you joy.

7. Legacy and Impact: Beyond personal growth, a long-term vision may involve leaving a positive legacy and making a meaningful impact on your community or the world. It encourages you to think beyond immediate goals and consider the long-lasting effects of your actions.

• Example: If your long-term vision includes contributing to mental health awareness, you might set goals related to advocacy, volunteering, or creating resources that benefit others.

Creating a long-term vision for personal and professional development provides you with a sense of purpose, motivation, and direction. It helps you make informed decisions, set meaningful goals, and navigate life's challenges with resilience. Ultimately, it serves as a powerful tool for shaping your journey toward improved mental well-being and a fulfilling life.

Section 2: Expanding Your Impact

This section explores ways to expand your impact by applying problem-solving skills to broader societal challenges.

Step 3: Identify New Challenges

Identify new challenges or causes that align with your values and expertise. Consider how your problem-solving skills can address these challenges.

To identify new challenges effectively:

• Research and Exploration: Explore areas where you can make a meaningful impact, whether it's in education, healthcare, environmental conservation, or social justice.

• Collaboration: Seek out collaborative opportunities with organizations and individuals already working on these challenges.

• Community Engagement: Engage with your local community to understand their needs and potential areas of improvement.

Step 4: Scale Your Efforts

Scaling your efforts involves expanding your initiatives to reach a wider audience and create a more significant impact.

To scale your efforts effectively:

- Strategic Planning: Develop a strategic plan that outlines how you will scale your initiatives, including resource allocation and timelines.

- Leverage Technology: Utilize technology and digital platforms to reach a broader audience and streamline processes.

- Partnerships: Form partnerships with organizations, governments, or community leaders to leverage their resources and expertise.

Section 3: Nurturing Resilience

Resilience is a cornerstone of sustaining growth and impact. This section explores strategies for nurturing resilience in the face of ongoing challenges.

Step 5: Resilience-Building Practices

Incorporate resilience-building practices into your daily life to maintain your capacity to overcome setbacks.

To nurture resilience effectively:

Nurturing resilience effectively involves developing a range of skills, strategies, and habits that enable you to bounce back from adversity, adapt to change, and thrive in the face of life's challenges. Here's an in-depth exploration of how to nurture resilience effectively:

1. Embrace a Growth Mindset: Cultivating a growth mindset is the foundation of resilience. It involves the belief that challenges are opportunities for growth and learning. When setbacks occur, view them as valuable experiences that can strengthen your resilience.

2. Build Emotional Intelligence: Understanding and managing your emotions is crucial for resilience. Develop emotional intelligence by recognizing and expressing your feelings in a healthy way. This includes practicing self-compassion and empathy for others.

3. Develop Problem-Solving Skills: Effective problem-solving is a key component of resilience. Learn how to break down complex issues into manageable parts, identify potential solutions, and take action. Problem-solving empowers you to regain control in challenging situations.

4. Foster Social Connections: Building and maintaining strong social connections is essential for resilience. Cultivate a support network of friends, family, and mentors who can provide emotional support and practical assistance during tough times.

5. Prioritize Self-Care: Self-care is not selfish; it's a vital aspect of resilience. Pay attention to your physical, mental, and emotional well-being. This includes getting adequate sleep, eating nourishing foods, engaging in regular exercise, and practicing relaxation techniques.

6. Cultivate Adaptability: Resilience involves adaptability to changing circumstances. Be open to adjusting your goals, strategies, and expectations when necessary. Flexibility allows you to navigate unexpected challenges more effectively.

7. Develop Coping Strategies: Identify healthy coping mechanisms that work for you. This may include mindfulness, deep breathing exercises, journaling, or seeking professional help when needed. Having a repertoire of coping strategies enhances your resilience toolkit.

8. Set Realistic Goals: Establish achievable goals that challenge you without overwhelming you. Setting small, manageable milestones allows you to experience a sense of accomplishment, which fuels resilience.

9. Practice Gratitude: Focusing on gratitude can boost your resilience. Regularly acknowledge and appreciate the positive aspects of your life, even during difficult times. Gratitude helps shift your perspective and build emotional resilience.

10. Learn from Adversity: View adversity as an opportunity for personal growth and learning. Reflect on past challenges and consider what you've gained from those experiences. This self-reflection enhances your ability to navigate future difficulties.

11. Seek Support when Needed: Resilience doesn't mean facing challenges alone. Recognize when you require professional support, such as therapy or counseling. Seeking help is a sign of strength and an essential step in nurturing resilience.

12. Maintain a Sense of Purpose: Having a clear sense of purpose and meaning in your life provides a source of motivation and resilience. Identify your values and passions and align your actions with them.

13. Build Self-Confidence: Self-confidence is closely linked to resilience. Cultivate self-belief by acknowledging your past achievements and reinforcing a positive self-image. Confidence enables you to tackle challenges with greater assurance.

14. Practice Mindfulness: Mindfulness techniques, such as meditation and deep breathing exercises, can enhance your ability to stay present and calm in the face of adversity. Mindfulness fosters emotional regulation and resilience.

15. Develop a Supportive Narrative: The way you perceive and frame your life's story can impact your resilience. Cultivate a narrative that

emphasizes your strengths, resilience, and ability to overcome challenges.

Nurturing resilience is an ongoing process that involves self-awareness, self-compassion, and continuous growth. By incorporating these strategies into your daily life, you can enhance your resilience effectively, allowing you to thrive even in the most challenging circumstances.

Step 6: Adapt and Evolve

Adaptability is essential for sustaining growth. Be open to evolving your strategies and approaches as circumstances change.

To adapt and evolve effectively:

• Feedback Loops: Create feedback loops to gather insights from stakeholders and make data-driven decisions.

• Continuous Learning: Keep learning and staying updated on best practices and emerging trends in your field.

• Scenario Planning: Develop contingency plans for potential challenges, ensuring you're prepared for various scenarios.

"Adapt and Evolve" is a critical component of building resilience and effectively managing life's challenges. It emphasizes the need to remain flexible and open to change, as well as the ability to adjust your strategies and mindset in response to evolving circumstances. Here's a detailed exploration of this step:

1. Embrace Change: Adaptability begins with acknowledging that change is a constant part of life. Whether it's a major life transition, unexpected setbacks, or daily fluctuations, understanding that change is natural can reduce resistance and anxiety.

2. Open-Mindedness: Being open to new ideas, perspectives, and possibilities is crucial for adaptability. An open-minded approach allows you to explore different solutions, consider alternative viewpoints, and discover opportunities in unexpected places.

3. Flexibility: Flexibility means being able to bend without breaking. It involves adjusting your plans, expectations, and behaviors when necessary. Flexibility enables you to navigate unforeseen challenges with grace and resilience.

4. Learn from Experience: Every experience, whether positive or negative, provides an opportunity for learning and growth. Embrace the lessons that come with challenges, and use them to inform your future decisions and actions.

5. Problem-Solving: Adaptation often requires problem-solving skills. When faced with a new situation or obstacle, approach it with a

structured problem-solving mindset. Break down complex issues into manageable components, identify potential solutions, and take action.

6. Emotional Regulation: Effective adaptability involves regulating your emotions. Practice emotional intelligence by recognizing and managing your feelings in response to change. Emotionally balanced responses help you make better decisions and maintain resilience.

7. Develop Coping Strategies: Build a toolbox of coping strategies that you can employ during times of change and uncertainty. These strategies might include mindfulness, relaxation techniques, seeking social support, or engaging in creative outlets.

8. Set Realistic Expectations: While adaptability is essential, it's also important to set realistic expectations for yourself. Understand that adaptation takes time and effort, and not every challenge can be overcome immediately. Be patient with yourself.

9. Self-Reflection: Periodically reflect on your adaptability skills and your responses to change. Self-reflection allows you to identify areas where you excel and areas that may require improvement. It also helps you stay aligned with your values and long-term goals.

10. Seek Support: During times of significant change or adversity, seeking support from friends, family, or a mental health professional

can be invaluable. Support networks provide emotional validation, guidance, and a sense of connection.

11. Maintain a Growth Mindset: A growth mindset entails the belief that you can develop and improve your abilities over time. Embrace challenges as opportunities for growth and view setbacks as stepping stones toward greater resilience.

12. Stay Adaptable Physically: Physical well-being plays a role in adaptability. Prioritize healthy habits such as regular exercise, a balanced diet, and adequate sleep. Physical health supports mental and emotional resilience.

13. Embrace Uncertainty: Understand that life is inherently uncertain. Embracing this uncertainty can reduce anxiety and fear associated with change. Focus on building the skills and mindset needed to navigate the unknown with confidence.

14. Celebrate Small Wins: Recognize and celebrate your successes, even if they are small. Acknowledging progress reinforces your ability to adapt and evolve, making you more resilient in the long run.

15. Create a Personal Growth Plan: Develop a plan for personal growth and adaptation. Set achievable goals and milestones that align with your long-term vision. Regularly revisit and adjust your plan as circumstances evolve.

Adaptability is a dynamic skill that strengthens with practice and self-awareness. By cultivating adaptability, you not only enhance your resilience but also increase your capacity to thrive in a rapidly changing world. It empowers you to face challenges with confidence and creativity, ultimately contributing to your personal growth and well-being.

Section 4: Conclusion and Looking Forward

In this concluding section of Chapter 11, we'll summarize the key takeaways and provide a glimpse of what to expect in the final chapter, where we'll explore the legacy of effective problem-solving and personal growth.

Step 7: Summary of Key Takeaways

Throughout this chapter, we've discussed strategies for sustaining personal growth, expanding impact, nurturing resilience, and adapting to ongoing challenges. Here are the key takeaways to remember:

- Reflection: Regularly reflect on your journey to sustain personal growth.

- New Goals: Set new goals that align with your evolving aspirations.

- Identify Challenges: Identify new challenges or causes that align with your values and expertise.

- Scale Efforts: Scale your initiatives to reach a wider audience and create a more significant impact.

- Nurture Resilience: Incorporate resilience-building practices into your life.

- Adapt and Evolve: Be open to adapting your strategies and approaches as circumstances change.

Step 8: Looking Forward to Chapter 12

As you conclude this chapter, consider your continued journey of growth, impact, and resilience. In Chapter 12, we'll explore the legacy of effective problem solving, the ripple effect it has on others, and how your journey can inspire and empower future generations.

Chapter 12: Leaving a Lasting Legacy

In Chapter 12, we'll dive into the concept of leaving a lasting legacy through effective problem solving and personal growth. We'll discuss:

- The ripple effect of your actions on others and the world.

- Strategies for mentoring and empowering future change agents.

- Reflecting on your journey and the impact you've had on your community and beyond.

Stay tuned for a meaningful exploration of the legacy you can create through your journey of personal growth and problem solving.

"You are never too old to set another goal or to dream a new dream." —C.S. Lewis

Chapter 12: Leaving a Lasting Legacy

Section 1: The Ripple Effect of Your Actions

This section explores how your actions and problem-solving efforts can have a profound ripple effect on others and the world.

Step 1: Recognizing the Ripple Effect

Every action you take, every problem you solve, and every positive change you create has a ripple effect that extends far beyond your immediate sphere.

To recognize the ripple effect effectively:

• Acknowledge Your Impact: Understand that your actions, whether small or large, influence others and the world.

• Stories of Inspiration: Seek out and reflect on stories of individuals whose actions created lasting change and inspired others.

• Empathy: Develop empathy for the people and communities your actions touch. Understand their needs and aspirations.

Step 2: Inspiring Change in Others

Your journey of personal growth and effective problem solving can serve as a powerful source of inspiration for others.

To inspire change in others effectively:

● Storytelling: Share your journey and experiences through powerful storytelling. Connect on a personal deep level with those who can learn from your path.

● Mentorship: Actively mentor and support individuals who aspire to make a positive impact. Provide guidance and share your knowledge.

● Lead by Example: Continue to lead by example in your community, home and beyond, by demonstrating the impact of effective problem solving.

Section 2: Strategies for Mentoring and Empowering Future Change Agents

This section we provide practical strategies for mentoring and empowering the next generation of change agents and problem solvers.

Step 3: Becoming a Mentor

Mentoring involves sharing your knowledge, experiences, and wisdom with others who aspire to make a difference.

To become a mentor effectively:

• Identify Mentees: It is important to identify individuals who show a genuine interest in your field or cause.

• Structured Guidance: Establish a structured mentoring relationship with clear objectives and expectations.

• Feedback and Encouragement: Provide constructive feedback and continuous encouragement to foster growth and engagement.

Step 4: Empowering Youth and Emerging Leaders

Empowering young individuals and emerging leaders is a key part of creating a lasting legacy.

To empower youth effectively:

• Education and Skill Development: Support educational programs and initiatives that develop problem-solving skills and leadership qualities.

• Youth Engagement: Engage with youth organizations, offering guidance and mentorship.

- Encourage Innovation: Encourage and celebrate young innovators and problem solvers who bring fresh perspectives to existing challenges.

Section 3: Reflecting on Your Journey

Reflecting on your journey of personal growth and problem solving is a vital step in understanding the legacy you've created.

Step 5: Legacy Reflection

Reflect on your journey and the impact you've had on your community and the world.

To reflect on your legacy effectively:

- Document Your Journey: Document your experiences, challenges, and successes in a format that future generations can learn from.

- Feedback and Evaluation: Seek feedback and evaluation from those who have been influenced by your actions. Understand how you've made a difference.

- Gratitude and Humility: Approach your legacy with gratitude and humility, recognizing the contributions of others along the way.

Section 4: Conclusion and Your Ongoing Legacy

In this concluding section of Chapter 12, we'll summarize the key takeaways and issue a call to action for readers to continue building their legacies through problem solving and personal growth.

Step 6: Summary of Key Takeaways

Throughout this chapter, we've explored the ripple effect of your actions, strategies for mentoring and empowering future change agents, and the importance of reflecting on your legacy. Here are the key takeaways to remember:

• Ripple Effect: Understand the profound impact your actions can have on others and the world.

• Inspire Change: Share your journey to inspire and motivate others to become change agents.

• Mentorship: Become a mentor and empower the next generation of problem solvers.

• Reflect on Your Legacy: Take time to reflect on your journey and the impact you've had.

As you conclude this chapter, consider how your legacy will continue to evolve and inspire future generations. Your problem-solving skills and personal growth journey have the potential to create a lasting positive impact on the world.

With this chapter, we've explored the concept of leaving a lasting legacy through problem solving, personal growth, and mentoring. If you have any additional sections, themes, or topics you'd like to explore or if you have any specific requests for the book's conclusion or any other aspects, please let me know, and I'll be happy to assist further.

Chapter 13: Conclusion and Your Ongoing Journey

Section 1: Reflecting on Your Journey

This section provides an opportunity for readers to reflect on their personal journeys of problem solving and growth.

Step 1: Your Journey in Review

It is vital to take a moment to review your personal journey. Reflect on the challenges you've overcome, the successes you've achieved, and the people who have supported you along the way.

To review your journey effectively:

- Timeline: Create a timeline of significant milestones in your problem-solving and personal growth journey.

- Lessons Learned: Identify the most valuable lessons you've learned from your experiences.

- Gratitude: Express gratitude for the opportunities, resources, and support that have been instrumental in your journey.

Step 2: Acknowledging Your Growth

Acknowledge the personal growth you've undergone throughout your journey. Consider how you've evolved as a problem solver and as an individual.

To acknowledge your growth effectively:

- Self-Reflection: Reflect on the changes in your mindset, skills, and perspectives.

- Feedback: Seek feedback from mentors, peers, and those you've mentored to gain insights into your growth.

- Future Aspirations: Consider how your growth can be applied to future endeavors and challenges.

Section 2: Your Ongoing Journey

This section emphasizes that personal growth and problem solving are ongoing processes. It encourages readers to embrace the journey ahead.

Step 3: Embracing Continuous Learning

Embrace the concept of continuous learning as a fundamental aspect of your ongoing journey.

To embrace continuous learning effectively:

- Learning Mindset: Maintain a growth mindset that thrives on acquiring new knowledge and skills.

- Reading and Resources: Explore books, articles, courses, and resources that align with your goals.

- Mentoring and Guidance: Seek ongoing mentorship and guidance to further develop your problem-solving capabilities.

Step 4: Setting New Goals

Set new goals and challenges that reflect your current aspirations and the impact you wish to make.

To set new goals effectively:

- Alignment with Values: Ensure that your goals align with your values and the legacy you want to create.

- S.M.A.R.T. Goals: Apply the SMART framework to set clear, achievable, and time-bound goals.

- Short-Term and Long-Term: Distinguish between short-term and long-term goals to create a balanced journey.

Section 3: Paying It Forward

This section emphasizes the importance of paying forward the knowledge, support, and inspiration you've received.

Step 5: Mentorship and Support

Continue to mentor and support others who are on their own journeys of problem solving and personal growth.

To provide mentorship and support effectively:

- Structured Mentorship: Develop structured mentoring relationships with individuals who can benefit from your guidance.

- Peer Support: Create peer support networks or communities where knowledge and experiences are shared.

- Leading by Example: Lead by example in your community by demonstrating the power of effective problem solving.

Step 6: Your Ongoing Legacy

Consider how your ongoing journey contributes to your legacy and the impact you leave on the world.

To build your ongoing legacy effectively:

- Legacy Goals: Define specific goals and actions that contribute to the legacy you want to leave.

- Evolving Impact: Be open to evolving the ways in which you make a positive impact on society and the world.

- Document Your Journey: Continue documenting your experiences and insights for future generations.

Section 4: Final Thoughts and Farewell

In this concluding section of Chapter 13, we'll summarize the key takeaways and bid farewell as readers embark on their ongoing journeys of problem solving and personal growth.

Step 7: Summary of Key Takeaways

Throughout this chapter, we've discussed the importance of reflecting on your journey, embracing continuous learning, setting new goals, paying it forward through mentorship and support, and considering your ongoing legacy. Here are the key takeaways to remember:

- Reflection: Reflect on your journey and acknowledge your growth.

- Continuous Learning: Embrace lifelong learning and personal development.

- New Goals: Set new goals that align with your current aspirations.

• Mentorship: Continue to mentor and support others on their journeys.

• Ongoing Legacy: Consider how your ongoing journey contributes to your legacy.

Step 8: Farewell and New Beginnings

As you conclude this book, remember that your journey of problem solving and personal growth is a lifelong adventure. Embrace new beginnings and the countless opportunities that await you.

Congratulations on completing these chapter so far on problem-solving skills and personal development.

Chapter 14: Developing Critical Thinking Skills

Section 1: Understanding Critical Thinking

This section introduces readers to the concept of critical thinking and its significance in problem solving and decision-making.

Critical thinking is crucial in problem-solving and decision-making for several reasons:

Effective Problem Identification:

• Critical thinking enables individuals to analyze situations objectively, identifying the root causes of problems rather than merely addressing symptoms. This leads to more effective problem-solving by tackling issues at their source.

Objective Analysis:

• It promotes a rational and unbiased assessment of information and evidence. Critical thinkers can evaluate data, arguments, and perspectives objectively, leading to more informed and logical decisions.

Informed Decision-Making:

- Critical thinking involves gathering relevant information, considering various perspectives, and weighing evidence before making decisions. This ensures that decisions are well-informed and based on a comprehensive understanding of the situation.

Creativity and Innovation:

- Critical thinking fosters creative thinking and innovation. It encourages individuals to explore alternative solutions, think outside the box, and consider unconventional approaches to problem-solving, leading to innovative and effective solutions.

Efficient Problem-Solving Process:

- Critical thinkers are adept at breaking down complex problems into manageable parts, allowing for a systematic and organized problem-solving process. This efficiency contributes to quicker and more effective solutions.

Risk Management:

- Critical thinking involves assessing potential risks and uncertainties associated with different decisions. This helps in developing strategies to mitigate risks, making decision-making more resilient and adaptive to changing circumstances.

Enhanced Communication:

• Individuals with strong critical thinking skills can articulate their thoughts, ideas, and decisions effectively. This improves communication within teams, facilitates collaborative problem-solving, and ensures that everyone involved is on the same page.

Continuous Improvement:

• Critical thinkers are inclined to reflect on their decisions and outcomes. This reflective process contributes to a culture of continuous improvement, where individuals learn from experiences, refine their problem-solving strategies, and strive for better results in the future.

Adaptability:

• Critical thinking equips individuals with the ability to adapt to changing circumstances. When faced with unexpected challenges, critical thinkers can analyze new information quickly, adjust their strategies, and make sound decisions in dynamic environments.

Ethical Decision-Making:

• Critical thinking involves ethical considerations, ensuring that decisions align with ethical standards and values. This ethical dimension is essential for responsible and socially conscious decision-making.

In summary, critical thinking is paramount in problem-solving and decision-making as it enhances analytical abilities, promotes informed choices, encourages creativity, and contributes to the overall effectiveness and adaptability of individuals and organizations.

Let's navigate some examples:

Medical Diagnosis:

• Scenario: A patient presents with a set of symptoms that do not fit a clear diagnostic pattern. The medical team needs to critically analyze the symptoms, consider various potential diagnoses, and conduct further tests to arrive at an accurate diagnosis.

Business Strategy Planning:

• Scenario: A company faces increased competition in its market. The leadership team must critically assess market trends, competitor strategies, and internal capabilities to formulate a strategic plan that ensures the company's long-term success and competitiveness.

Legal Decision-Making:

- Scenario: Lawyers working on a complex legal case need to critically evaluate evidence, precedents, and legal arguments to build a strong case for their clients. Critical thinking is essential for constructing persuasive legal strategies and anticipating potential counterarguments.

Engineering Problem-Solving:

- Scenario: Engineers working on a construction project encounter unexpected challenges due to soil conditions. They must critically assess the situation, analyze geological data, and adapt their designs to ensure the structural integrity and safety of the project.

Educational Curriculum Design:

- Scenario: Educators developing a curriculum for a diverse group of students need to critically analyze educational theories, consider different learning styles, and adapt teaching methods to create an inclusive and effective learning environment.

Environmental Conservation:

- Scenario: Environmental scientists facing the challenge of preserving a delicate ecosystem must critically evaluate the impact of human activities, assess biodiversity, and develop conservation strategies that balance ecological sustainability with human needs.

Global Crisis Response:

• Scenario: During a global crisis, such as a pandemic, leaders in healthcare, government, and international organizations need to critically analyze epidemiological data, assess healthcare infrastructure, and make decisions that prioritize public health while considering economic and social implications.

Technology Development:

• Scenario: Engineers developing new technologies must critically assess the potential ethical implications, environmental impact, and societal consequences of their innovations. This critical thinking is crucial for responsible and sustainable technological advancements.

Journalistic Investigation:

• Scenario: Journalists investigating a complex story need to critically analyze information sources, verify facts, and discern the credibility of their findings. Critical thinking is essential for presenting accurate and unbiased news reports.

Military Strategy:

• Scenario: Military leaders planning strategic operations must critically assess intelligence reports, anticipate enemy movements, and make decisions that consider geopolitical factors. Critical thinking is crucial for effective military planning and execution.

These real-life examples illustrate the diverse range of situations where critical thinking is essential across various fields and professions. It involves analyzing information, solving complex problems, making informed decisions, and adapting strategies to address challenges effectively.

Developing strong critical thinking skills offers a multitude of benefits, particularly in the areas of decision-making and problem-solving. Here are key advantages:

Enhanced Decision-Making:

• Clarity in Choices: Critical thinkers can sift through information, identify relevant details, and discern the most important factors in a decision, leading to clearer and more informed choices.

• Informed Decision-Making: With the ability to critically evaluate options, individuals can make decisions based on a deeper understanding of the situation, reducing the likelihood of impulsive or uninformed choices.

• Risk Management: Critical thinking helps individuals assess risks associated with different decisions, allowing for better risk management and the development of strategies to mitigate potential negative outcomes.

Improved Problem-Solving:

• Effective Problem Identification: Critical thinkers excel at recognizing the root causes of problems, addressing issues at their source rather than treating symptoms. This leads to more effective and sustainable problem-solving.

• Creative Solutions: Strong critical thinking fosters creativity and innovation in problem-solving. Individuals can explore unconventional approaches, think outside the box, and develop creative solutions to complex challenges.

• Systematic Approach: Critical thinkers employ a systematic approach to problem-solving, breaking down complex issues into manageable parts. This structured method enhances the efficiency and effectiveness of the problem-solving process.

Increased Analytical Abilities:

• Objective Analysis: Critical thinking encourages individuals to analyze information objectively, avoiding biases and emotional influences. This results in more accurate assessments and conclusions.

- Data Interpretation: Individuals with strong critical thinking skills can interpret data more effectively, extracting meaningful insights and making data-driven decisions.

Adaptability to Change:

- Flexibility: Critical thinkers are more adaptable to change. They can analyze new information quickly, adjust strategies, and make sound decisions in dynamic and evolving situations.

- Resilience: The ability to think critically enhances resilience in the face of challenges. Individuals can navigate uncertainties with confidence and adapt their problem-solving approaches as needed.

Effective Communication:

- Articulation of Ideas: Critical thinkers can articulate their thoughts, ideas, and decisions clearly and persuasively, facilitating effective communication within teams and organizations.

- Collaborative Problem-Solving: Teams with members who possess strong critical thinking skills can collaborate more effectively in problem-solving, leveraging diverse perspectives to reach innovative solutions.

Continuous Improvement:

- Reflective Practice: Critical thinkers engage in reflective practice, learning from experiences and continuously improving their problem-solving strategies over time.

- Professional Growth: Developing and applying critical thinking skills contributes to ongoing professional growth, as individuals refine their abilities and stay abreast of evolving challenges and opportunities.

In summary, the benefits of strong critical thinking skills extend across decision-making and problem-solving, offering individuals and organizations a competitive edge in navigating complexities and achieving success.

Step 2: The Role of Critical Thinking in Problem Solving

Critical thinking plays a pivotal role in effective problem-solving by providing individuals with a systematic and rational approach to challenges. Here's an illustration of how critical thinking is an integral part of the problem-solving process:

Problem Identification:

- Without Critical Thinking:

- Individuals might focus on surface-level symptoms, addressing only the immediate issues without understanding the underlying causes.

- With Critical Thinking:

- Critical thinkers analyze the situation objectively, asking questions to uncover the root causes of the problem. They go beyond the obvious symptoms to understand the complexities involved.

Analysis of Information:

- Without Critical Thinking:

- Individuals may rely on assumptions or accept information at face value without questioning its validity.

- With Critical Thinking:

- Critical thinkers carefully analyze information, considering its source, relevance, and reliability. They question assumptions and seek evidence to support their understanding of the problem.

Identifying Patterns and Trends:

- Without Critical Thinking:

- Individuals may struggle to identify patterns or trends in the data, missing important connections.

- With Critical Thinking:

- Critical thinkers excel at recognizing patterns and trends, allowing them to see the bigger picture. This enables a more comprehensive understanding of the problem and potential solutions.

Generating Alternative Solutions:

- Without Critical Thinking:

- Individuals might settle for the first solution that comes to mind without exploring alternatives.

- With Critical Thinking:

- Critical thinkers engage in divergent thinking, generating multiple alternative solutions. They weigh the pros and cons of each option, considering potential outcomes and implications.

Evaluating Options:

- Without Critical Thinking:

- Individuals may lack a systematic approach to evaluating options, making decisions based on personal biases or emotions.

- With Critical Thinking:

- Critical thinkers use objective criteria to evaluate options. They consider the feasibility, impact, and ethical implications of each solution, ensuring a thorough and rational decision-making process.

Implementing Solutions:

- Without Critical Thinking:

- Individuals may struggle to implement solutions effectively, encountering unforeseen challenges.

- With Critical Thinking:

- Critical thinkers anticipate potential obstacles and develop contingency plans. Their systematic approach ensures a smoother implementation of chosen solutions.

Reflecting on Outcomes:

- Without Critical Thinking:

- Individuals might neglect to reflect on the outcomes, missing valuable insights for future problem-solving.

- With Critical Thinking:

- Critical thinkers engage in reflective practice, analyzing the outcomes of their decisions. This reflection informs continuous improvement, refining their problem-solving skills over time.

In essence, critical thinking acts as a guiding framework throughout the problem-solving process. It empowers individuals to approach challenges with a rational mindset, ensuring a thorough understanding of the problem, the generation of creative and effective solutions, and a continuous learning process for future problem-solving endeavors.

To emphasize the role of critical thinking effectively:

Critical thinking is a fundamental component that enhances every stage of the problem-solving process. Let's explore how critical thinking contributes to each stage:

Defining the Problem:

- Without Critical Thinking:

- Individuals may define the problem based on surface-level symptoms, leading to a superficial understanding.

- With Critical Thinking:

- Critical thinkers approach problem definition with precision, asking probing questions to uncover the root causes. They consider various perspectives, ensuring a comprehensive understanding of the problem.

Analyzing the Situation:

- Without Critical Thinking:

- Individuals may accept information at face value, lacking a thorough analysis of relevant data and factors.

- With Critical Thinking:

- Critical thinkers analyze information critically, questioning assumptions, verifying data, and considering the credibility of sources. This analytical depth provides a solid foundation for problem-solving.

Identifying Potential Causes:

- Without Critical Thinking:

- Individuals might focus on the most obvious causes, overlooking nuanced or interconnected factors.

- With Critical Thinking:

- Critical thinkers delve deeper into the situation, identifying potential causes by considering patterns, relationships, and the interplay of various elements. They avoid simplistic explanations and embrace complexity.

Generating Alternative Solutions:

- Without Critical Thinking:

- Individuals may settle for the first solution that comes to mind, limiting creativity and innovation.

- With Critical Thinking:

- Critical thinkers employ divergent thinking, generating a wide range of alternative solutions. They explore unconventional ideas, fostering creativity and ensuring a more comprehensive set of options.

Evaluating Options:

- Without Critical Thinking:

- Individuals may lack a systematic approach to evaluating options, relying on personal biases or incomplete criteria.

- With Critical Thinking:

- Critical thinkers use objective criteria to evaluate options. They consider factors such as feasibility, ethical considerations, and potential consequences. This ensures a thorough and rational decision-making process.

Selecting a Solution:

- Without Critical Thinking:

- Individuals might make decisions impulsively or based on emotions, neglecting a careful consideration of the best course of action.

- With Critical Thinking:

- Critical thinkers make decisions based on a careful analysis of the available information. They weigh the strengths and weaknesses of each solution, considering both short-term and long-term implications.

Implementing the Solution:

- Without Critical Thinking:

- Individuals may encounter unforeseen challenges during implementation due to a lack of strategic planning.

- With Critical Thinking:

- Critical thinkers anticipate potential obstacles and develop a detailed implementation plan. They consider various contingencies, ensuring a smoother execution of the chosen solution.

Reflecting on the Outcome:

- Without Critical Thinking:

- Individuals may neglect to reflect on the outcomes, missing valuable insights for future problem-solving.

- With Critical Thinking:

- Critical thinkers engage in reflective practice, analyzing the outcomes of their decisions. This reflection informs continuous improvement, refining their problem-solving skills over time.

In summary, critical thinking acts as a guiding force throughout the problem-solving process. It ensures a thorough and systematic approach at every stage, leading to more effective and sustainable solutions. Critical thinkers bring depth, creativity, and adaptability to the problem-solving process, enhancing their ability to address complex challenges successfully.

Open-mindedness is a crucial attribute that significantly enhances the quality of thinking and decision-making. Here's why fostering an open mind is essential:

Embracing Diversity of Thought:

• Open-minded individuals appreciate diverse perspectives and understand that solutions to complex problems often arise from a collective exchange of ideas. They welcome input from different viewpoints, fostering a rich pool of ideas.

Enhanced Problem-Solving:

• Open-mindedness allows for a more comprehensive exploration of potential solutions. By considering a range of perspectives, individuals can identify innovative and unconventional approaches to problem-solving that may not be apparent with a closed mind.

Adaptability to Change:

• An open mind enables individuals to adapt to changing circumstances more effectively. When faced with new information or unexpected challenges, open-minded individuals are more likely to adjust their thinking and strategies, ensuring greater resilience in dynamic environments.

Improved Decision-Making:

• Considering multiple perspectives provides a more holistic view of a situation, enabling individuals to make well-informed decisions. Open-mindedness mitigates the risk of making decisions based on biases or incomplete information.

Conflict Resolution:

• Open-mindedness is key to resolving conflicts. By understanding and acknowledging diverse viewpoints, individuals can find common ground and work toward mutually beneficial solutions. This approach fosters positive relationships and collaboration.

Continuous Learning:

• Open-minded individuals have a natural inclination for continuous learning. They seek out new information, welcome feedback, and adapt their beliefs based on evolving knowledge. This commitment to learning enhances personal and professional growth.

Creativity and Innovation:

• Creativity thrives in an environment where different ideas are encouraged. Open-mindedness fuels innovation by allowing individuals to connect seemingly unrelated concepts, leading to the development of novel solutions and approaches.

Effective Communication:

• An open mind facilitates effective communication. Individuals who are receptive to diverse perspectives can articulate their ideas more clearly and engage in constructive dialogue. This promotes a positive and collaborative communication culture.

Building Strong Relationships:

• Open-mindedness is a foundation for building strong relationships, both personally and professionally. It fosters empathy, understanding, and respect for others' opinions, creating an environment of trust and cooperation.

Global Perspective:

• In an interconnected world, an open mind is essential for understanding different cultures, perspectives, and global issues. It promotes a global mindset, enabling individuals to navigate the complexities of a diverse and interconnected society.

In essence, open-mindedness is a catalyst for growth, collaboration, and effective problem-solving. It not only enriches individual thinking but also contributes to the creation of inclusive and innovative environments where diverse talents and ideas can thrive. Embracing open-mindedness is a powerful step toward personal and collective success.

Data-driven decisions are at the heart of critical thinking, representing a strategic and informed approach to problem-solving. Here's why integrating data and evidence is a fundamental aspect of critical thinking:

Objective Analysis:

- Critical thinking involves an objective and unbiased analysis of information. Data provides an empirical foundation for this analysis, allowing individuals to assess situations without being swayed by personal biases or emotions.

Evidence-Based Understanding:

- Critical thinkers rely on evidence to form a comprehensive understanding of a problem or situation. Data serves as the evidence that supports or challenges assumptions, ensuring a more accurate and reliable foundation for decision-making.

Informed Decision-Making:

• Integrating data into the decision-making process ensures that choices are based on a thorough understanding of the situation. This evidence-based approach minimizes the risk of making decisions solely on intuition or incomplete information.

Risk Assessment:

• Critical thinkers use data to assess risks associated with different options. By quantifying potential outcomes and understanding the likelihood of specific scenarios, individuals can make decisions that are more resilient to uncertainties and unforeseen challenges.

Precision in Problem-Solving:

• Data allows for precise problem definition and identification of root causes. Critical thinkers leverage data to pinpoint specific issues, guiding the development of targeted and effective solutions.

Comparative Analysis:

• Data enables individuals to compare and contrast different options systematically. Critical thinkers can weigh the pros and cons of each alternative, ensuring a more thorough evaluation and selection process.

Continuous Improvement:

- Critical thinkers engage in a continuous improvement cycle, where data on outcomes is analyzed to refine strategies. This iterative process ensures that decisions are adaptive and based on real-world results.

Quantitative and Qualitative Insights:

- Critical thinking involves considering both quantitative and qualitative data. This holistic approach provides a more nuanced understanding of the problem, allowing individuals to factor in both the statistical significance and the human elements involved.

Communication of Findings:

- Critical thinkers use data to communicate their findings effectively. Whether presenting solutions to a team or stakeholders, data-driven insights provide a clear and compelling rationale for the chosen course of action.

Predictive Analysis:

- Critical thinking involves anticipating future scenarios. Data-driven decisions incorporate predictive analysis, where historical and current data are used to forecast potential outcomes and trends, allowing individuals to proactively address emerging challenges.

In summary, critical thinking and data-driven decision-making are intertwined concepts. By embracing data and evidence, critical thinkers enhance their ability to analyze situations objectively, make informed decisions, and continuously refine their approaches based on real-world results. This approach not only strengthens individual decision-making skills but also contributes to the overall effectiveness of organizations and teams.

Section 2: Developing Critical Thinking Skills

This section provides practical strategies and exercises for readers to develop and enhance their critical thinking skills.

Unlocking Critical Thinking Through Active Listening:

Active listening is a transformative skill that forms the bedrock of critical thinking. By engaging in intentional and focused listening, individuals can enrich their understanding, cultivate empathy, and elevate their problem-solving capabilities. Here's why and how you should make active listening a cornerstone of your daily interactions:

Deepening Understanding:

• Active listening involves not just hearing but truly comprehending the message being conveyed. By immersing yourself in the speaker's words, you gain a deeper understanding of their perspectives, concerns, and insights.

Empathy Building:

• Understanding others' viewpoints is essential for critical thinking. Active listening fosters empathy, allowing you to step into the speaker's shoes and appreciate the nuances of their experiences. This empathetic connection enhances your ability to consider diverse perspectives when approaching problems.

Uncovering Implicit Messages:

• People often convey implicit messages through tone, body language, or subtle cues. Active listening enables you to pick up on these nuances, helping you grasp the full context of a conversation. This skill is invaluable for critical thinkers seeking a comprehensive understanding of complex situations.

Clarifying Assumptions and Biases:

• Actively listening prompts you to question your assumptions and biases. As you absorb information without immediate judgment, you create space for self-reflection. This self-awareness is crucial for critical thinkers aiming to approach problems with an open and unbiased mindset.

Enhancing Communication Skills:

• Effective communication is a two-way street, and active listening is a key component. By honing your active listening skills, you not only receive information more accurately but also communicate more effectively. This contributes to a collaborative problem-solving environment.

Building Trust and Rapport:

• Trust is foundational for teamwork and collaboration. Active listening demonstrates respect and genuine interest, fostering trust and rapport with others. A trusting environment is conducive to open discussions, diverse idea sharing, and ultimately, more effective critical thinking.

Reducing Misunderstandings:

• Misunderstandings can derail problem-solving efforts. Active listening minimizes the risk of misinterpretation by ensuring that you grasp the speaker's intended message. This clarity is essential for making well-informed decisions.

Encouraging Inclusive Participation:

• Critical thinking thrives in diverse and inclusive environments. Active listening encourages everyone to contribute their perspectives, ensuring that a wide range of ideas is considered. This inclusive participation enriches the problem-solving process.

Practice Active Listening Daily:

• Silence Distractions: In a world filled with distractions, commit to minimizing external interruptions when engaging in conversations. Turn off electronic devices, set aside dedicated time, and create a focused environment for active listening.

• Maintain Eye Contact: Visual cues are powerful. Maintain eye contact with the speaker to convey your attentiveness and signal that you are fully engaged in the conversation.

• Ask Clarifying Questions: Seek clarification when needed to ensure that you have accurately understood the speaker's message. This not only demonstrates your commitment to understanding but also clarifies any potential points of confusion.

• Paraphrase and Summarize: Periodically paraphrase or summarize what you've heard. This not only reinforces your understanding but also shows the speaker that you are actively processing the information.

• Demonstrate Non-Verbal Engagement: Use non-verbal cues such as nodding, smiling, and mirroring to signal your engagement and encouragement. Non-verbal communication enhances the overall quality of the interaction.

Incorporating active listening into your daily interactions is a powerful catalyst for unlocking critical thinking. It enriches your understanding, cultivates empathy, and creates a collaborative environment where diverse perspectives can flourish. As you embrace active listening, you embark on a journey of continuous learning, self-reflection, and heightened problem-solving prowess.

Practicing Active Listening Effectively: Unlocking the Power of Engagement, Questioning, and Summarization

Active listening is a dynamic skill that goes beyond merely hearing words—it involves full engagement, thoughtful questioning, and strategic summarization. Here's why and how you can practice these key elements to become a more effective active listener:

1. Engagement: The Heart of Active Listening

Being fully engaged in conversations is paramount for active listening. It's more than just being physically present; it's about dedicating your attention, showing genuine interest, and creating a space for meaningful connection. Here's why engagement matters:

- Fostering Connection:

- Engagement builds a bridge of connection between you and the speaker. It communicates that you value their thoughts and perspectives, creating a conducive environment for open dialogue.

- Demonstrating Respect:

- Your engagement is a powerful indicator of respect. It acknowledges the speaker's importance and signals that you are committed to understanding their message without distractions or preoccupations.

- Non-Verbal Cues:

- Non-verbal cues, such as maintaining eye contact, nodding, and using affirmative gestures, convey your engagement. These cues reassure the speaker that their words are being received with attention and consideration.

- Preventing Misunderstandings:

• Full engagement minimizes the risk of misunderstandings. By immersing yourself in the conversation, you are better equipped to grasp the nuances of the speaker's message, reducing the chance of misinterpretation.

Practice Tip: Dedicate specific time slots for focused conversations, eliminate distractions, and actively participate in the dialogue by responding with relevant comments and feedback.

2. Questioning: The Gateway to Deeper Understanding

Asking thoughtful questions is a powerful tool for delving deeper into the speaker's thoughts and gaining a comprehensive understanding. Here's why questioning is a key aspect of active listening:

• Encouraging Elaboration:

• Thoughtful questions prompt the speaker to elaborate on their ideas, providing additional context and details. This enriches your understanding and allows for a more nuanced perspective.

• Clarifying Ambiguities:

• Questions serve as a mechanism to clarify any ambiguities or uncertainties in the speaker's message. They demonstrate your commitment to accuracy and a genuine desire to comprehend the information correctly.

- Expressing Interest:

- Asking questions conveys your interest in the conversation. It shows that you are actively thinking about the topic and seeking to uncover deeper layers of information.

- Creating Dialogue:

- Questions transform the conversation into a dialogue. This interactive exchange of ideas fosters a collaborative environment where both parties contribute to the exploration of the topic.

Practice Tip: Develop the habit of asking open-ended questions that encourage the speaker to share more details. Listen actively to their responses and use follow-up questions to explore specific aspects further.

3. Summarization: Ensuring Comprehension and Connection

Summarizing what you've heard is a vital step in the active listening process. It solidifies your understanding, provides clarity, and reinforces your connection with the speaker. Here's why summarization holds significant value:

- Affirming Understanding:

- Summarizing demonstrates that you've actively processed the information and understood the key points. It serves as a checkpoint to ensure that both parties are on the same page.

- Enhancing Retention:

- The act of summarization improves information retention. By distilling the essential elements of the conversation, you create mental landmarks that contribute to a more enduring memory of the discussion.

- Facilitating Feedback:

- Summarizing allows you to provide feedback to the speaker. It offers an opportunity to affirm areas of agreement, seek clarification on potential misunderstandings, and contribute your reflections to the ongoing dialogue.

- Encouraging Further Exploration:

- A well-crafted summary can pave the way for deeper exploration of specific points. It invites the speaker to share additional insights or elaborate on aspects that may require more attention.

Practice Tip: Practice the art of concise summarization by capturing the main ideas and key takeaways from a conversation. Use phrases like "If I understand correctly..." to initiate your summaries.

Incorporating engagement, questioning, and summarization into your active listening practice transforms it from a passive activity into a dynamic skill set. By honing these elements, you not only enhance your understanding of others but also contribute to a more collaborative and effective communication environment. Remember, active listening is not just about hearing; it's about truly connecting with the speaker and unlocking the power of shared insights.

Step 4: Analyze and Evaluate Information

Navigating the Information Landscape: A Guide to Critical Analysis and Evaluation

In an era of information overload, the ability to analyze and evaluate information critically is paramount. It empowers individuals to sift through the vast sea of data, discern credible sources from misinformation, and make informed decisions. Here's a guide to honing your skills in source evaluation, bias recognition, and comparative analysis:

1. Source Evaluation: Verifying Credibility

Importance of Source Evaluation:

- Reliability and Accuracy:

- Ensure that information comes from reputable sources known for accuracy and reliability. Look for publications, journals, or organizations with a track record of producing trustworthy content.

- Expertise and Authority:

- Assess the expertise and authority of the author or organization behind the information. Experts in a field or institutions with a strong reputation are more likely to provide reliable insights.

- Publication Date:

- Consider the publication date of the information. In rapidly evolving fields, recent data may be crucial, while in others, historical context might be relevant. Be mindful of outdated information.

- Transparency and Citations:

- Credible sources are transparent about their information-gathering methods and provide citations to support their claims. Check for references and cross-verify information where possible.

Practice Tip: Develop a habit of checking the credentials of authors and the publishing platform. Be wary of information lacking clear attribution or from sources with a history of disseminating misleading content.

2. Bias Recognition: Unmasking Perspectives

Teaching Bias Recognition:

• Identifying Implicit Bias:

• Recognize that bias can be implicit and unintentional. Be aware of your own biases and understand how they might influence your interpretation of information.

• Diverse Perspectives:

• Seek information from diverse sources to obtain a well-rounded view. Recognize that bias can manifest not only in the content but also in the selection and framing of information.

• Language and Tone:

• Analyze the language and tone used in the information. Be cautious of emotionally charged language, as it may indicate a bias or an attempt to sway opinions.

- Consider the Agenda:

- Understand the potential agenda of the information source. Some sources may have a specific viewpoint or agenda that can shape the narrative. Evaluate how this might impact the information presented.

Practice Tip: Actively seek out information from sources with differing perspectives. Compare how different outlets cover the same topic to identify potential biases.

3. Comparative Analysis: Weighing Perspectives

Encouraging Comparative Analysis:

- Multiple Sources:

- Consult multiple sources to gain a comprehensive understanding. Compare how different sources report the same information and identify commonalities or disparities.

- Cross-Verification:

- Cross-verify facts and claims across different platforms. Reliable information should be consistent across reputable sources.

- Evaluate Counterarguments:

- Consider alternative viewpoints and counterarguments. Critical analysis involves understanding multiple perspectives and being open to reassessing your own views.

- Fact-Checking Tools:

- Leverage fact-checking tools and websites to verify information. These tools can help you quickly assess the accuracy of claims and statements.

Practice Tip: Create a habit of consulting multiple sources before forming conclusions. Actively seek out perspectives that challenge your initial assumptions to foster a well-informed perspective.

Conclusion:

In the age of information overload, mastering the art of critical analysis and evaluation is a skill that empowers individuals to navigate the complexities of the digital landscape. By honing your ability to assess sources, recognize bias, and conduct comparative analyses, you become a discerning consumer of information, equipped to make informed decisions in a world rich with data and perspectives.

Section 3: Problem-Solving and Decision-Making

Step 5: Define the Problem Clearly - The Cornerstone of Effective Problem-Solving

In the intricate dance of problem-solving, the spotlight shines brightly on the pivotal Step 5: Define the Problem Clearly. This foundational step is not merely a formality but rather the compass that sets the course for the entire problem-solving journey. Here's why defining the problem with precision is of paramount importance:

**1. Clarity Illuminates the Path:

•   Why it Matters:

•   Defining a problem with clarity is akin to turning on a light in a dimly lit room. It illuminates the intricacies, allowing you to see the contours of the challenge before you. Without clarity, you risk stumbling in the dark, addressing symptoms rather than root causes.

•   How it Enhances Critical Thinking:

•   Clear problem definition is a testament to critical thinking prowess. It involves dissecting the complexity, understanding the nuances, and distilling the challenge into its essential components. This precision reflects a thoughtful and analytical approach.

357

**2. Guiding the Solution Journey:

- Why it Matters:

- A well-defined problem acts as a guiding star for the solution journey. It provides a roadmap, steering you away from aimless efforts and towards targeted interventions. Without this roadmap, you risk meandering through potential solutions without a clear destination.

- How it Enhances Critical Thinking:

- Critical thinkers approach problem definition with a strategic mindset. They ask probing questions, uncover layers of complexity, and distinguish between symptoms and root causes. This analytical depth ensures that the defined problem aligns with the true nature of the challenge.

**3. Setting Realistic Goals:

- Why it Matters:

- Clear problem definition lays the groundwork for setting realistic goals. It enables you to establish achievable milestones and benchmarks for success. Without this clarity, goals may be arbitrary or misaligned with the actual problem.

- How it Enhances Critical Thinking:

- Critical thinkers are adept at setting SMART goals—Specific, Measurable, Achievable, Relevant, and Time-bound. They align these goals with the intricacies of the defined problem, ensuring a targeted and effective problem-solving process.

**4. Focused Problem-Solving:

- Why it Matters:

- A clear problem definition focuses your problem-solving efforts. It helps you allocate resources, time, and energy where they are most needed. Without this focus, you risk scattering efforts across various aspects of the challenge, diluting the impact of your interventions.

- How it Enhances Critical Thinking:

- Critical thinkers thrive in focused problem-solving environments. They resist the temptation to address peripheral issues and, instead, channel their analytical skills into dissecting and understanding the core problem. This focused approach is a hallmark of critical thinking in action.

**5. Avoiding Assumptions and Biases:

- Why it Matters:

- Clear problem definition prompts a critical examination of assumptions and biases. It challenges preconceived notions, ensuring that your understanding of the problem is not clouded by unfounded beliefs. Without this scrutiny, assumptions can lead you astray, and biases can shape a distorted problem definition.

- How it Enhances Critical Thinking:

- Critical thinkers approach problem definition with a keen awareness of potential biases and assumptions. They interrogate their own perspectives and actively seek diverse viewpoints to ensure a more objective and comprehensive understanding of the problem.

Conclusion:

In the intricate tapestry of problem-solving, defining the problem clearly is the thread that weaves together precision, focus, and strategic thinking. It is the hallmark of a critical thinker—a navigator who understands that the success of the entire journey hinges on the clarity with which the problem is articulated. As you embark on your problem-solving endeavors, remember: the more precisely you define the problem, the more effectively you set the stage for innovative solutions and informed decision-making.

Mastering Effective Problem Definition: Crafting a Clear Problem Statement, Root Cause Analysis, and Goal Setting

In the intricate dance of problem-solving, the overture begins with the precision of your problem definition. Let's delve into the key components of this process:

1. Problem Statement: Crafting Clarity in Conciseness

Importance:

- A concise problem statement is the compass that guides your problem-solving efforts. It succinctly captures the essence of the challenge, providing a focal point for analysis and intervention.

How to Create a Concise and Specific Problem Statement:

Be Specific:

- Clearly articulate the problem without ambiguity. Avoid vague language and strive for specificity to ensure a targeted understanding of the issue.

Focus on the Issue, Not Symptoms:

- Identify the core problem rather than its symptoms. Symptoms are manifestations of the underlying issue; addressing them directly may provide temporary relief but won't lead to a sustainable solution.

Quantify Where Possible:

- Whenever feasible, quantify the aspects of the problem. Numbers add precision and help in setting measurable goals. For instance, instead of stating a general decline in productivity, specify the percentage decrease.

Use Clear Language:

- Choose language that is clear and easily understandable. Avoid jargon or technical terms that might obscure the meaning for those not intimately familiar with the issue.

Practice Tip: Imagine explaining the problem to someone who has no prior knowledge of the situation. If they can grasp the issue from your description, your problem statement is on the right track.

2. Root Cause Analysis: Digging Beneath the Surface

Importance:

- Identifying root causes is the difference between treating symptoms and solving problems at their core. It prevents the recurrence of issues and forms the basis for effective solutions.

Emphasizing the Importance of Identifying Underlying Causes:

Ask "Why" Iteratively:

- Utilize the "5 Whys" technique. Ask "Why" repeatedly to peel back the layers of symptoms until you uncover the fundamental, underlying causes of the problem.

Distinguish Between Causes and Effects:

- Differentiate between causes and effects. Causes are the origins of the problem, while effects are the visible outcomes. Focusing on causes ensures long-term resolution.

Use Fishbone Diagrams:

- Create fishbone diagrams (Ishikawa diagrams) to visually map out potential causes and their relationships. This tool helps in systematically exploring factors contributing to the problem.

Consider Interconnections:

• Recognize that causes are often interconnected. Addressing one cause might impact others, so a holistic approach is essential.

Practice Tip: When identifying a cause, assess whether addressing it directly would eliminate the problem or significantly contribute to its resolution. If not, continue probing for deeper causes.

3. Goal Setting: Charting the Course for Success

Importance:

• Clear objectives provide a roadmap for your problem-solving journey. They serve as benchmarks for success and guide your efforts in a focused and measurable direction.

Encouraging Clear Objectives for Problem Resolution:

Use SMART Criteria:

• Employ the SMART criteria for goal setting—Specific, Measurable, Achievable, Relevant, and Time-bound. This ensures your objectives are clear, quantifiable, and aligned with your problem statement.

Align Goals with Root Causes:

- Ensure your goals directly address the root causes identified during the analysis. This alignment strengthens the likelihood of achieving a sustainable solution.

Prioritize Goals:

- If multiple goals are identified, prioritize them based on their impact on the core problem. This helps in directing resources and attention effectively.

Periodic Evaluation and Adjustment:

- Regularly assess progress toward your goals and be willing to adjust them if necessary. Flexibility ensures your objectives remain relevant in dynamic problem-solving scenarios.

Practice Tip: If your goal is specific and measurable, envision what success would look like. If you can visualize the outcome, it's a strong indicator that your goal is well-defined.

Conclusion:

In the art of problem-solving, the precision of your problem definition sets the stage for success. Crafting a clear problem statement, conducting root cause analysis, and setting tangible goals are the brushstrokes that shape the canvas of your solution. As you embark on your problem-solving journey, remember: the clarity with which you define the problem determines the effectiveness of your interventions.

Step 6: Generate and Evaluate Solutions - A Roadmap for Critical Decision-Making

As you stand at the crossroads of problem-solving, Step 6 beckons you to not only generate solutions but to scrutinize them with a critical eye. Let's navigate through the art of brainstorming, criteria-based evaluation, and rational decision-making:

1. Brainstorming: Cultivating Creativity for Solutions

Why Brainstorming Matters:

• Brainstorming is the fertile ground where creativity flourishes, yielding a plethora of potential solutions. It encourages free thinking, diverse perspectives, and the exploration of unconventional ideas.

Brainstorming Techniques:

Free-Form Brainstorming:

• Allow participants to freely express ideas without immediate judgment. Encourage quantity over quality initially to stimulate creativity.

Mind Mapping:

• Create a visual representation of ideas, linking related concepts. This technique helps in exploring the interconnections between different solutions.

Round-Robin Brainstorming:

• Facilitate a structured discussion where each participant contributes one idea in turn. This ensures equal participation and prevents dominant voices from overshadowing others.

Reverse Brainstorming:

• Instead of generating solutions, focus on identifying ways to exacerbate the problem. This unconventional approach can often lead to innovative problem-solving insights.

Practice Tip: Set a time limit for brainstorming sessions to maintain focus and encourage rapid idea generation.

2. Criteria-Based Evaluation: Weighing the Pros and Cons

Why Criteria-Based Evaluation Matters:

- Establishing criteria for solution evaluation brings order to the array of ideas. It provides a systematic framework for assessing each solution's merits and drawbacks.

Establishing Criteria for Evaluation:

Relevance to the Problem:

- Assess how directly each solution addresses the defined problem. Solutions should align with the root causes and contribute to comprehensive resolution.

Feasibility:

- Evaluate the practicality of each solution. Consider factors such as available resources, time constraints, and potential obstacles that may impact implementation.

Cost-Benefit Analysis:

- Weigh the costs against the benefits for each solution. This analysis helps in prioritizing solutions that offer the greatest impact relative to their resource requirements.

Alignment with Goals:

- Ensure that each solution aligns with the goals set during problem definition. This alignment ensures a cohesive and focused problem-solving strategy.

Practice Tip: Collaborate with team members or stakeholders to establish evaluation criteria. This collective input ensures a comprehensive and diverse perspective.

3. Rational Decision-Making: Guiding Choices with Logic

Why Rational Decision-Making Matters:

- Rational decision-making steers you away from impulsive choices, grounding your selections in evidence and logic. It transforms the evaluation process into a strategic and objective decision-making journey.

Encouraging Rational Decision-Making:

Gather and Analyze Information:

- Ensure you have comprehensive information about each solution. Analyze data, consider expert opinions, and gather insights to inform your decision-making.

Consider Risks and Benefits:

- Evaluate the potential risks associated with each solution alongside their benefits. A balanced assessment ensures a well-informed decision that anticipates potential challenges.

Avoid Emotional Bias:

- Acknowledge and set aside emotional biases when making decisions. Emotional responses can cloud judgment, and rational decision-making requires a clear and objective mindset.

Prioritize Solutions:

- Based on the evaluation criteria, prioritize solutions that align most closely with your goals and offer the highest probability of success.

Practice Tip: Create a decision matrix that assigns weights to each criterion and scores each solution accordingly. This systematic approach adds a quantitative dimension to the decision-making process.

Conclusion:

In the realm of problem-solving, the journey from brainstorming to decision-making is a symphony of creativity and logic. As you traverse Step 6, remember that the solutions you generate and evaluate are the building blocks of your resolution. By cultivating a creative atmosphere, establishing robust evaluation criteria, and making decisions rooted in logic, you pave the way for effective and impactful problem-solving.

Section 4: Conclusion and Ongoing Practice

Step 7: Summary of Key Takeaways - Nurturing Your Critical Thinking Journey

As we conclude this chapter, let's distill the essence of our exploration into key takeaways that serve as guideposts on your critical thinking journey:

1. Definition of Critical Thinking:

- Analyzing, Evaluating, Synthesizing:

Critical thinking is the art of systematically analyzing, evaluating, and synthesizing information. It involves going beyond surface-level understanding to make informed and thoughtful decisions.

2. Role in Problem Solving:

- Rational Analysis and Decision-Making:

Critical thinking is the linchpin in the machinery of problem-solving. It elevates the process by infusing it with rational analysis, enabling more precise problem definition, and guiding decisions based on evidence and logic.

3. Key Critical Thinking Skills:

- Active Listening:

The foundation of critical thinking lies in active listening. By fully engaging in conversations and absorbing information, you set the stage for robust analysis and understanding.

- Information Analysis:

Scrutinizing information with a discerning eye is a fundamental critical thinking skill. It involves separating facts from opinions, recognizing biases, and ensuring a thorough examination of data.

- Problem Definition:

Precision in problem definition is a hallmark of critical thinking. Clarity in articulating the problem ensures that subsequent steps in the problem-solving process are focused and effective.

- Solution Evaluation:

The ability to evaluate potential solutions systematically is a critical thinking skill that rounds out the problem-solving process. Criteria-based evaluation and rational decision-making are key components.

4. Benefits of Developing Critical Thinking Skills:

• Improved Decision-Making:

Strengthening your critical thinking skills directly contributes to enhanced decision-making. By grounding choices in evidence and logic, you navigate complexities with clarity and confidence.

• Effective Problem-Solving:

A robust set of critical thinking skills transforms problem-solving into a strategic and purposeful endeavor. It equips you to dissect challenges, define problems with precision, and evaluate solutions with a discerning eye.

Conclusion: Continue Your Critical Thinking Journey:

• Practice and Development:

The journey of critical thinking is a continuous evolution. Embrace opportunities to practice and refine your skills. Engage in active listening, hone your information analysis abilities, and consistently apply critical thinking to real-world scenarios.

- Curiosity and Open-Mindedness:

Cultivate curiosity and maintain an open-minded approach. Critical thinking thrives in an environment where diverse perspectives are considered, and assumptions are regularly challenged.

- Lifelong Learning:

Recognize that critical thinking is a lifelong learning process. Stay curious, seek new challenges, and approach problems with the mindset of a perpetual learner.

As you carry these key takeaways forward, remember that critical thinking is not just a skill set; it's a mindset—an approach to navigating the complexities of the world with clarity, curiosity, and a commitment to informed decision-making. May your journey be enriched with the continuous cultivation of your critical thinking skills.

Step 8: Ongoing Practice - Cultivating Critical Thinking as a Daily Habit

As we draw the curtains on this chapter, let's underscore the enduring nature of critical thinking and the significance of ongoing practice. Here's a heartfelt encouragement to fuel your journey:

1. Consistent Application in Daily Life:

- Integrate Critical Thinking Daily:

Make critical thinking an integral part of your daily life. Apply it not just to solve problems but also to enhance your understanding of the world around you.

- Reflect on Daily Decisions:

Take moments to reflect on your daily decisions. Consider how critical thinking could have influenced certain choices, and identify areas for improvement.

2. Seeking Opportunities for Growth:

- Embrace Challenges:

View challenges as opportunities to exercise and grow your critical thinking muscles. Approach problems with curiosity and a willingness to learn.

- Diversify Experiences:

Seek diverse experiences and perspectives. Exposing yourself to different viewpoints broadens your understanding and fosters a more inclusive and comprehensive approach to critical thinking.

3. Continuous Learning and Adaptation:

- Stay Inquisitive:

Cultivate a mindset of continuous learning. Stay curious, ask questions, and remain open to new information and insights.

- Adapt to Change:

Critical thinking thrives in dynamic environments. Embrace change as an opportunity to apply your skills in adapting to new circumstances and finding innovative solutions.

4. Connect with Fellow Critical Thinkers:

- Engage in Discussions:

Connect with others who value critical thinking. Engage in discussions, share perspectives, and learn from each other's approaches to problem-solving.

- Build a Learning Community:

Foster a community of learners who encourage and challenge each other. Collaborative critical thinking enhances the richness of perspectives and solutions.

Conclusion: A Lifelong Journey of Growth:

- Embrace the Journey:

Remember that developing critical thinking is a journey, not a destination. Embrace the process of growth, acknowledging that each challenge and triumph contributes to your evolving skillset.

- Celebrate Progress:

Celebrate the progress you make along the way. Every instance where you consciously apply critical thinking is a step toward honing a valuable and empowering skill.

In closing, let this chapter mark the beginning of a continuous and enriching journey. May your commitment to ongoing practice elevate your critical thinking skills, enabling you to navigate challenges with clarity, wisdom, and a steadfast commitment to thoughtful decision-making. Here's to a future brimming with growth, curiosity, and the enduring pursuit of excellence in critical thinking.

Author's Final Words

As we reach the end of this transformative journey, I want to express my deepest gratitude for joining me on this path of personal growth and resilience. Throughout this book, we've explored the intricacies of unleashing your inner resilience for the sake of personal growth and mental well-being. It's been an incredible privilege to be your guide, and I hope the insights and strategies shared here have empowered you to embark on your unique journey of self-discovery and empowerment.

Remember that your journey is a story in progress, and each chapter brings new opportunities for growth and learning. Your inner resilience is a wellspring of strength that will continue to empower you as you face life's challenges, embrace change, and pursue your dreams with unwavering determination.

As the author, my greatest hope is that you carry forward the wisdom you've gained from these pages and apply it to your life in meaningful ways. Share your story of growth and resilience with others, for it is through our shared experiences that we inspire and uplift those around us.

Your future is brimming with possibilities, and I encourage you to continue nurturing your personal growth, fostering resilience, and thriving in every facet of your life. The journey may have reached its conclusion here, but your path to self-discovery and empowerment is an ever-unfolding adventure. Embrace it with open arms, a resilient heart, and the unwavering belief that you have the power to create a future filled with fulfillment, purpose, and boundless joy.

Thank you for entrusting me with a part of your journey. May your life be a testament to the incredible resilience and strength that resides within you.

With heartfelt gratitude,

Belladonna Sterling

Psychologist

Printed in Great Britain
by Amazon